ALIEN WISDOM

THE LIMITS OF HELLENIZATION

Alien Wisdom

THE LIMITS OF HELLENIZATION

ARNALDO MOMIGLIANO

PROFESSOR OF ANCIENT HISTORY, UNIVERSITY COLLEGE LONDON

CAMBRIDGE UNIVERSITY PRESS

CAMBRIDGE

LONDON · NEW YORK · MELBOURNE

Published by the Syndics of the Cambridge University Press
The Pitt Building, Trumpington Street, Cambridge CB2 1RP
Bentley House, 200 Euston Road, London NW1 2DB
32 East 57th Street, New York, NY 10022, USA
296 Beaconsfield Parade, Middle Park, Melbourne 3206, Australia

First published 1975

Printed in Great Britain by
Western Printing Services Ltd
Bristol

Library of Congress Cataloguing in Publication Data

Momigliano, Arnaldo.
Alien Wisdom.

Includes bibliographies and index.
1. Civilization, Greek – Foreign influences –
Addresses, essays, lectures. I. Title.
DF78.M6   938   75-10237
ISBN 0 521 20876 9

Contents

Per mia madre,
presente sempre nel suo vigile amore
(Torino 1884 – campo nazista di sterminio 1943)

Ps. 79.2–3

Preface

The substance of this book was presented as the Trevelyan Lectures in the University of Cambridge in May 1973 and in a revised form as the A. Flexner Lectures at Bryn Mawr College in February–March 1974. I have retained the lecture form and only added a bibliography to each chapter. My aim was to stimulate discussion on an important subject without indulging in speculations.

I owe much gratitude to the two institutions which invited and received me so generously. In Cambridge I found myself among old friends: at Bryn Mawr I gained new ones. It was a happy time in both places. I should like to thank especially Professors Owen Chadwick and M. I. Finley of Cambridge, President Wofford, Professor Agnes Michels and Professor Russell Scott of Bryn Mawr.

A.M.

University College London
August 1974

I

The Greeks and their neighbours
in the Hellenistic world

PRELIMINARY CONSIDERATIONS

I

The philosophic historian will never stop meditating on the nose of Cleopatra. If that nose had pleased the gods as it pleased Caesar and Antony, a loose Alexandrian gnosticism might have prevailed instead of the Christian discipline imposed by the two Romes, the old one on the Tiber, and the new one on the Bosporus. The Celts would have been allowed to go on collecting mistletoe in their forests. We would have fewer books on Queen Cleopatra and on King Arthur, but even more books on Tutankhamen and on Alexander the Great. But a Latin-speaking Etruscologist, not a Greek-speaking Egyptologist, brought to Britain the fruits of the victory of Roman imperialism over the Hellenistic system. We must face the facts.

The victory of Roman imperialism can in its turn be described as the result of four factors: the new direction given by Rome to the social – that is the military – forces of old Italy; the utter inability of any Hellenistic army to match the Romans in the field; the painful erosion of Celtic civilization and its appendages which went on for centuries and ultimately enabled the Romans to control the resources of western Europe from the Atlantic to the Danubian regions; and finally the co-operation of Greek intellectuals with Italian politicians and writers in creating a new bilingual culture which gave sense to life under Roman rule. Only the Jews and the Iranians stood up to the Romans, as they had stood up to the Seleucids. The Jews had not a chance, but in the course of their toils one of their minority groups acquired autonomy and challenged the Roman Empire in a more fundamental manner than the old worshippers of the Temple of Jerusalem had ever done. As for the Arsacid dynasty of Parthia, it claimed its independence about 247 B.C. and made good its word. For nine centuries Iran remained free. Not only its army, but its religious tradition was a force to be reckoned with.

Four of the five protagonists of this story – Greco-Macedonians, Romans, Jews and Celts – came together for the first time in the Hellenistic period. Indeed for all practical purposes the Greeks discovered Romans, Celts and Jews only after Alexander the Great. There is an element of paradox in this. Greek colonies had prospered in Italy not very far from Rome for centuries. Massalia had been in direct contact with the Celts at least since the fifth century B.C. The Jews lived in a region where Greek mercenaries were often stationed and Greek merchants often called. The Iranians, who soon freed themselves from Hellenistic control and always escaped that of Rome, were also the only nation which the Greeks had known and appraised before Alexander. The Persian Empire was indeed another story altogether: it had ruled over Greeks. But even for the Iranians the Hellenistic era meant a change in appreciation: the prophet Zoroaster took the place of King Cyrus as the most characteristic Iranian figure. Rome replaced Persia as the empire by which the Greeks were directly challenged. Parthia was by now a remote state, though formidable: the Magi had some of the prestige of the mysterious region from which they came and offered spiritual goods of their own.

Thus the Hellenistic age saw an intellectual event of the first order: the confrontation of the Greeks with four other civilizations, three of which had been practically unknown to them before, and one of which had been known under very different conditions. It seemed to me that the discovery of Romans, Celts and Jews by the Greeks and their revaluation

of Iranian civilization could be isolated as the subject of these
Trevelyan lectures. The details are not well known, nor is
the general picture clear. There are of course things to be
said also about Egypt and Carthage. Hermes Trismegistus
emerged from Egypt more or less at the time in which
Zoroaster and the Magi became respected figures among the
Greeks: they will have to be considered together. In both
cases the Platonic school played an essential part. Though
Plato never made it explicit that Thoth, the inventor of
science, was identical with Hermes, the identification is
stated by Aristoxenus of Tarentum and Hecataeus of Abdera
(Stobaeus 1, *Prooem.* 6, p. 20 Wachsmuth = Aristoxenus
fr. 23 Wehrli; Diodorus 1.16). The search for cultural heroes
and religious guides was never confined to one country only.
It already embraced Brahmans, Magi, Egyptian priests and
Druids by the beginning of the second century B.C., as we
know from the authors quoted by Diogenes Laertius in his
prooemium. The group went on growing until St Augustine,
or rather his source, made it include all the barbarians:
'Atlantici Libyes, Aegyptii, Indi, Persae, Chaldaei, Scythae,
Galli, Hispani' (*Civ. dei* 8.9). Two considerations, however,
have persuaded me to leave Egypt on the periphery of my
enquiry: (1) Egypt had interested the Greeks since Homer
as a country difficult to approach and with puzzling customs.
It was never treated as a political power. If anything, it was
a repository of unusual knowledge. Herodotus gave two
ultimately contradictory reasons for spending so much of his
time on it, first that 'the Egyptians in most of their manners
and customs exactly reverse the common practice of mankind' (2.35), and secondly that the Greeks derived so many
of their religious and scientific notions from the Egyptians
that even those 'that are called followers of Orpheus and of
Bacchus are in truth followers of the Egyptians and of Pythagoras' (2.81). There was therefore no dramatic change in the
Greek evaluation of Egypt during the Hellenistic period,
though the rise of Hermes Trismegistus as a god of knowledge was new. (2) Native Egyptian culture declined during

the Hellenistic period because it was under the direct control
of Greeks and came to represent an inferior stratum of the
population. The 'hermetic character of the language and of
the script', as Claire Préaux called it (*Chron. d'Égypte* 35
(1943), 151), made the Egyptian-speaking priest – not to
mention the peasant – singularly unable to communicate with
the Greeks. The creation of Coptic literature in the new conditions of Christianity indicates the vitality of this underground culture. But the Hellenistic Greeks preferred the
fanciful images of an eternal Egypt to the Egyptian thought
of their time.

Carthaginian culture, on the other hand, did not decline:
it was murdered by the Romans, who, quite symbolically,
donated the main library of Carthage to the Numidian Kings
(Plin. *N.H.* 18.22). I would gladly talk about the ideas of
the Carthaginians, if we only knew them. Carthage, like the
Phoenician cities of Syria, had become increasingly Hellenized. Aristotle had treated Carthage at length as a Greek
polis. About 240–230 B.C. Eratosthenes put together Carthaginians, Romans, Persians and Indians as the barbarian
nations that came closest to the standards of Greek civilization and specified that Carthaginians and Romans were the
best governed (Strabo 1.4.9, p. 66).

In the second Punic War Hannibal had the support of
Greek historians, such as Silenus of Caleacte and Sosylus of
Sparta, and of course made an alliance with Philip V of
Macedonia. In the next lecture I shall produce some evidence
that about 190–185 B.C. there were many in Greece who
looked at Hannibal as a possible saviour from the Romans.
Vilification of the character of the Carthaginians was to be
found in the Sicilian-born historian Timaeus even before
some Roman orators and writers made '*Punica fides*' into a
catchword. But it is doubtful whether many Greeks were
taken in by such propaganda. Polybius refused to believe it
(cf. for instance, 9.26.9; 31.21.6). Notwithstanding Cato
and Cicero, and perhaps Ennius, there were even Latin
writers who refused to join in the chorus: there is nothing

4

very wrong in the *Poenulus* of Plautus; Cornelius Nepos wrote a most sympathetic sketch of Hannibal; Virgil came near to transferring '*Punica fides*' to Aeneas. Only Greek imperial writers such as Plutarch and Appian accepted what had become the conventional literary description of the Carthaginians without reflecting that '*Punica fides*' had its counterpart in '*Graeca fides*'. During the second century B.C. there must have been a feeling of common danger and interests between Greeks and Carthaginians. It was re-inforced by the considerable contribution to Greek philo-sophy by men of Phoenician stock. Iamblichus gives names of Carthaginian Pythagoreans (*Vita Pythagor.* 27.128; 36.267). One of the few circumstantial items of information we have suggests that if the Romans had not destroyed Carthage the Carthaginian intellectuals, like the Greek intellectuals, would have become pro-Roman. A young Carthaginian called Has-drubal came to Athens about 163 and joined the Academy under Carneades three years later. He became famous under the Greek name of Clitomachus and in 127 was recognized as the official head of his school. He dedicated books to L. Censorinus, consul 149, and to the poet Lucilius: he praised or perhaps adulated Scipio Aemilianus about 140. It does not contradict his devotion to the Romans that he should write a consolation for the Carthaginians after the destruction of the city in 146. Cicero still read this work (*Tuscul.* 3.54); and, being rather thick-skinned in these matters, did not feel the horridness of the situation. One wonders where the Carthaginians were to whom Clitomachus distributed his consolation. He had been caught in the spiral which made his contemporary Polybius the champion of Roman law and order. Another of these stray Carthaginians who wandered between Greece and Rome in the second century B.C. is probably to be recognized in Procles, son of Eucrates, a Carthaginian, whom Pausanias quotes twice. From one quotation (4.35.4) we learn that Procles compared Alexander with Pyrrhus and found the former superior in fortune, but the latter a better tactician. In the other quotation (2.21.6) he appears to have taken the Gorgon Medusa killed by Perseus as a member of a wild Libyan race: 'he (Procles) had seen a man from this race brought to Rome'. The Greek-sounding name of Procles and his father are more probably signs of Hellenization than of Greek origin. Procles was using his wits in the sort of intellectual games – rationalistic interpretations of myths, comparisons of popular military leaders – which appealed to the Greek and Roman public. He, too, in a more trivial way, seems to have been caught in the Greco-Roman spiral. Unfortunately, there is not enough evidence to make a coherent account of how Carthaginians and Greeks saw each other in the third and second centuries B.C. and how Rome came to profit from the situation – not least by the importation of an African slave who became the most accomplished of the Hellenized dramatists of Latin literature, Terence.

I shall therefore devote the substance of my lecture to a study of the cultural connections between Greeks, Romans, Celts, Jews and Iranians in the Hellenistic period. I shall go back into the classical age of Greece only in so far as it is necessary in order to understand the later times. What I want to ascertain is how the Greeks came to know and evaluate these groups of non-Greeks in relation to their own civilization. I expected to find interdependence, but no uniformity, in the Greek approach to the various nations and in the response of these nations (when recognizable from our evidence) to the Greek approach. What I did not expect to find – and what I did find – was a strong Roman impact on the intellectual relations between Greeks and Jews or Celts or Iranians as soon as Roman power began to be felt outside Italy in the second century B.C. The influence of Rome on the minds of those who came into contact with it was quick and strong.

II

Hellenistic civilization remained Greek in language, customs and above all in self-consciousness. The tacit assumption in Alexandria and Antioch, just as much as in Athens, was the superiority of Greek language and manners. But in the third and second centuries B.C. trends of thought emerged which reduced the distance between Greeks and non-Greeks. Non-Greeks exploited to an unprecedented extent the opportunity of telling the Greeks in the Greek language something about their own history and religious traditions. That meant that Jews, Romans, Egyptians, Phoenicians, Babylonians and even the Indians (Asoka's edicts) entered Greek literature with contributions of their own: what Xanthus did for the Lydians in the fifth century B.C. became a routine performance. More foreign gods were admitted into the Greek pantheon than at any time since prehistory. In their turn the barbarians not only accepted Greek gods, but assimilated many of their own gods to Greek gods. It was an unsystematic syncretism which was particularly successful in Italy (Etruria and Rome), left its mark on Carthage, Syria and Egypt, was unsuccessful in Judaea, rather insignificant in Mesopotamia, and affected at least the iconography, if not the substance, of Indian religion through Gandhara art. The notion of a barbaric wisdom gained consistency and acceptance among those who considered themselves Greeks. As early as the fifth and fourth centuries B.C. the Greek philosophers and historians had shown a keen interest in foreign doctrines and customs and had been inclined to recognize some value in them. The story of Pythagoras' studies with barbarian teachers is already to be found in fourth-century sources and may be older. Hermes Trismegistus, Zoroaster and his Magi, and to a lesser degree Moses and Abraham became respected figures with doctrines of their own on the operations of nature. The intellectual influence of the barbarians was, however, felt in the Hellenistic world only to the extent to which they were capable of expressing themselves in Greek. No Greek read the

7

Upanishads, the Gathas and the Egyptian wisdom books. It was indeed very difficult to find somebody non-Jewish reading the Bible in Greek even when it was made available in that language. Greek remained the only language of civilization for every Greek-speaking man. Even in the first century A.D. the author of the *Periplus maris Erythraei* cannot find a better accomplishment for a king of Ethiopia – to counterbalance his notorious greed for money – than his knowledge of Greek. The Jew Philo celebrated Augustus for extending the territory of Hellenism (*Leg. ad Gaium* 147).

The effort of the natives to be heard by the Greeks was evidently encouraged by the curiosity of the Greeks about the natives and, generally speaking, corresponded to the political situation. But the Greeks were seldom in a position to check what the natives told them: they did not know the languages. The natives on the other hand, being bilingual, had a shrewd idea of what the Greeks wanted to hear and spoke accordingly. This reciprocal position did not make for sincerity and real understanding. When there was no urgency, utopia and idealization abounded; where there was an immediate purpose, propaganda, adulation and reciprocal accusations prevailed. Nevertheless, the Mediterranean world had found a common language, and with it went a literature which was uniquely open to all sorts of problems, debates and emotions.

The novelty of such a situation will be more apparent if we compare with it what can be called the classical situation of the ancient world between 600 and 300 B.C. It has become a commonplace, after Karl Jaspers' *Vom Ursprung und Ziel der Geschichte* – the first original book on history to appear in post-war Germany in 1949 – to speak of the *Achsenzeit*, of the axial age, which included the China of Confucius and Lao-Tse, the India of Buddha, the Iran of Zoroaster, the Palestine of the Prophets and the Greece of the philosophers, the tragedians and the historians. There is a very real element of truth in this formulation. All these civilizations display literacy, a complex political organization combining central government and local authorities, elaborate town-planning, advanced metal technology and the practice of international diplomacy. In all these civilizations there is a profound tension between political powers and intellectual movements. Everywhere one notices attempts to introduce greater purity, greater justice, greater perfection and a more universal explanation of things. New models of reality, either mystically or prophetically or rationally apprehended, are propounded as a criticism of, and alternative to, the prevailing models. We are in the age of criticism – and social criticism transpires even from the involuted imagery of Zoroaster's Gathas. The personality of the critics is bound to emerge: they are the masters whose thoughts still count today and whose names we remember.

It is not for me here to try to account for the common features of movements so different in nature as those we have mentioned. What matters to us is that they were independent of each other and, to the best of our knowledge, ignored each other. During the Persian Empire Aramaic did not function as an international language in the same way in which Greek did in the period after Alexander. Aramaic did not penetrate deeply into Greece or Italy. There are exceptions. I would take as one of them the letters in Assyrian characters sent from Persia to Sparta which the Athenians intercepted and managed to translate in 425 B.C.: for surely by *Assyria grammata* Thucydides must mean an Aramaic text (4.50). If Democritus, who was supposed to have appropriated the sayings of Aḥiqar, was not in fact acquainted with them, at least Theophrastus was (Diog. Laert. 5.50; Clem. Alex. *Stromata* 1.15.69). But the amount of Aramaic literature which went into international circulation must have been limited in quantity and variety. The mixture of Hebrew and Aramaic we find in two books of the Bible implies that, at least among the Jews, Aramaic was written for no more international a public than that capable of reading Hebrew. True enough, even while using Greek, the Jews remained only too often bilingual for their own consumption, but the extent of their apologetic production in Greek indicates that they

aimed at Gentile readers. I cannot see any intention of this
kind in the Books of Ezra and Daniel.

The *Achsenzeit*, the axial age, is the development of several
civilizations on parallel lines. Characteristically, the *Achsenzeit* is not centred on Mesopotamia and Egypt, two civilizations which were very much in touch with each other and
with Persia, Judaea and Greece. But Mesopotamia and Egypt
still lived in a world which had been built in the second
millennium upon the power of monarchy – the divinely pro-
tected monarchy of Mesopotamia and the divine monarchy
of Egypt. They did not have to face protests and reforms in
the middle of the first millennium B.C. In Egypt a morality of
silence prevailed, and Mesopotamia – whether Assyria or
Chaldaea – seems to have been bent on conquering the others
rather than on criticizing herself. The men of Greece, Judaea,
Iran, India and China who transformed their countries
through their criticisms of the traditional order did not communicate with one another and did not create an international civilization. What constitutes the novelty of the
Hellenistic age is that it gave international circulation to
ideas, while strongly reducing their revolutionary impact.
Seen in comparison with the preceding axial age, the Hellenistic age is tame and conservative. Until St Paul arrives on
the scene, the general atmosphere is one of respectability.

What accentuates the peculiar physiognomy of Hellenistic
civilization is the special role two foreign groups – Jews and
Romans – came to play in it. The Jews basically remained
convinced of the superiority of their beliefs and ways of life
and fought for them. Yet they continuously compared their
own ideas with Greek ideas, made propaganda for their own
beliefs, absorbing many Greek notions and customs in the
process – and ultimately found themselves involved in that
general confrontation of Greek and Jewish values which we
call Christianity. The Romans never took their intellectual
relations with Hellenism so seriously. They acted from a
position of power and effortlessly preserved a strong feeling
of their own identity and superiority. They paid the Greeks

to teach them their wisdom and often did not even have to
pay because they were their slaves. However, by assimilating
and making their own so many Greek gods, literary conventions, artistic forms, philosophical ideas and social customs, they put themselves and the Greeks in a unique
reciprocal situation; the more so because they made their
own language an instrument of thought which could rival
Greek and render Greek ideas with remarkable precision
(though the Greeks never quite accepted the fact). No other
ancient language succeeded in doing this. It was not purely
a consequence of the similarity between Indo-European languages, for Celtic, Persian, Sanskrit and Pali were also Indo-
European. Since the third century B.C. there had been a
Latin Hellenism, never identical with the Greek, but never
separable from it. The people who created it made themselves
the masters of the Greek-speaking world within two centuries. After that the distinction between Greek and Roman
Hellenism remained valid, but there was no political barrier
between the two, and the Christian revolution involved both.

The comparison between the axial age and the Hellenistic
age also serves to remind us that Hellenism still affects our
attitude towards ancient civilizations. Since the time of Attila
many factors have contributed to the erosion of the Hellenistic
view of the world, but *homo Europaeus* has remained intellectually conditioned by his Hellenistic ancestors. The
triangle Greece–Rome–Judaea is still at the centre and is
likely to stay at the centre as long as Christianity remains
the religion of the West. Persia, Mesopotamia and Egypt
remain more or less where Hellenistic erudition put them as
the holders of barbarian wisdom. The Phoenicians, and in
particular the Carthaginians, are still given pride of place in
our handbooks for their institutions and their colonization
because the Greeks recognized themselves in such things.
The Celts, who were only superficially touched by Hellenistic
civilization and represented the greatest terror for both
Greeks and Romans, have simply been left outside the
horizon of the traditional civilized Western world. The

picture we give of them is still that of Posidonius. Vercin-
getorix, Boudicca and a few Druids are allowed to remind
the schoolboys of the European community that the Celts did
exist in the age of the Romans. The average knowledge of an
educated modern man about India is not superior to that
which is to be found in Greek and Roman writers. Even now
there is no obligation in our traditional curriculum to know
anything about China because the Greeks and the Romans
knew nothing or almost nothing about it. The eighteenth
century performed the greatest rescue operation for forgotten
civilizations humanity had ever witnessed. The Chinese, the
Indians and the Celts were the most important beneficiaries.
But the consequences were felt only by professors, philosophers, poets and cranks. Hellenistic culture interfered with
the parallel developments of individual cultures which had
extended from China to Greece in previous centuries. It
recognized and at the same time limited the importance of
Egypt, Mesopotamia and above all Iran. It created a privi-
leged situation of mutual stimulation and challenge between
Greeks and Romans and, in a more limited area, between
Jews and Greeks.

III

It is the special situation of the Romans in this triangle that
deserves the greatest attention, and it will come first in our
consideration. There was no challenge in the earliest relations
between Romans and Greeks. Monarchic Rome lived under
the influence of Etruscan culture, and Etruscan culture
absorbed a vast amount of Greek goods. Every new archaeological discovery emphasizes the close contacts of Greeks
with Etruscans in the sixth century. The latest revelation is
the Greek settlement at Graviscae, one of the harbours of
Caere, with its temple and its Greek votive offering by
Sostratus of Aegina. We now know where this man made his
money: in Italy, not at Tartessus, as had erroneously been
deduced from Herodotus 4.152.

The case of Etruria warns us that the assimilation of many

techniques and notions does not necessarily imply a real understanding between two civilizations. The Etruscans remained mysterious to the Greeks – one of the many reasons why they are still mysterious to us. If the Romans had followed the Etruscan path, Heraclides Ponticus would not have called Rome a Greek city, a *polis hellenis,* as early as the middle of the fourth century B.C. (Plut. *Cam.* 22). The same idea may have been implied by Aristotle when he attributed the foundation of Rome to Achaeans returning from Troy (Dionys. Hal. 1.72.3). Stories about some kinship between Romans and Greeks gained credit because Demetrius Poliorcetes referred to the 'kinship between Romans and Greeks' when he protested at Rome against the pirates of Antium – probably after 295 B.C. (Strabo 5.3.5, p. 232). Two contrasting features mark the relations between Rome and the Greek world during the fifth and fourth centuries B.C. On the one hand commercial relations must have decreased because there were fewer Greek imports than in the sixth century. The metropolitan Greeks noticed Rome only as a city in the dim distance. And even the western Greeks, with the exception of Massalia, paid very little attention to her. The annalistic tradition has few facts to relate; a few purchases of corn in times of famine, and the offer to Delphi after the destruction of Veii. No Greek writer travelled to Rome, and no Greek historian told her history at any length. On the other hand, the social development of Rome separated her from Etruria and made her similar to a Greek city; and this is what Heraclides Ponticus recognized.

The Servian centuriate organization – whether or not inspired by the Solonian model of the four classes – made Rome a timocratic city. The XII Tables – whether or not modelled on Greek legislation – provided Rome with a written constitution of the Greek type. The emancipation of the *plebs* and its progressive participation in the government seem to have no parallel in Etruria but are easily comprehensible in Greek terms. What is more, the Roman *plebs* seems to have taken a special interest in Greek religious and moral notions.

The temple of Ceres – Demeter – which was dedicated in 493 B.C. was regarded as the plebeian sanctuary; it was decorated by Greek artists and had a Greek priestess (Plin. *N.H.* 35.154; Cic. *Pro Balbo* 55). The establishment of the mixed patrician–plebeian collegium of the *Xviri sacris faciundis* coincides with the full parification of the two orders in the Licinian-Sextian laws of 367 B.C. The members of the college presumably had to know some Greek if they were to consult the Sibylline books. Finally, it is curious that the first two Greek cognomina in Roman onomastics belong to two plebeian consuls: Q. Publilius Philo, consul 339 and 327 B.C., and P. Sempronius Sophus, consul 304 B.C. Whether the introduction of the Greek cult of Apollo into Rome about 435 was due to plebeian initiative is a question to which there is no answer. Rome obviously had magistrates capable of dealing with the Greeks on proper diplomatic lines when she became involved with them during the conquest of southern Italy in the last decades of the fourth century. About 333 Rome made some sort of treaty with Alexander the Molossian during his Italian campaign; his sudden disappearance deprived the event of its potential importance. Seven years later Naples became an ally of Rome *aequo iure*. Significantly, it was the consul with a Greek surname, Q. Publilius Philo, who was entrusted with the drive into Campania which led to this pact in 326.

Rome, not Greece, prepared the conditions which were to make the relations between them such a unique affair. The Greeks did not go beyond that minimum of attention which their position demanded. Not surprisingly they noticed the sack of Rome by the Gauls, because Massalia could not overlook such a movement of Celtic populations and because the invaders were a danger to Magna Graecia too, besides being used by Dionysius I as mercenaries. The Romans decided to find out about the Greeks, tried to learn the language, accepted Greek gods and reshaped their constitution on lines which some Greeks recognized as akin to their own constitutions. At the end of the fourth century the very aristocratic

Fabii, who had so far been known as experts in the Etruscan language and in Etruscan affairs, decided to turn to Greek language and art and to diplomacy in the Hellenic world. What made C. Fabius Pictor paint the temple of Salus in 302 B.C. – 'sordidum studium' (Val. Max. 8.14.6) – is anybody's guess. But in 273 two of the three ambassadors to Ptolemy Philadelphus were Fabii (Val. Max. 4.3.9).

The Greeks did not react – or rather did not go beyond the surface of Roman life – until they found themselves faced with a first-class power which had defeated the Greek armies of Pyrrhus on the open field. The Ptolemies, being the neighbours of the Carthaginians who were the allies of the Romans, were the first Hellenistic kings to try to make friends with the unexpected new power. Timaeus, a Sicilian historian albeit resident in Athens, was the first to collect extensive information on the past of the Romans. He was not the first to be interested in Rome; certainly Theophrastus and perhaps Callias of Syracuse preceded him. His contemporary, Hieronymus of Cardia, had an excursus on Rome in his history of the Diadochi. But nobody else, to the best of our knowledge, gave so much attention and so much space to Rome as Timaeus; and nobody else was so influential. He had a date of his own for the foundation of Rome, made direct enquiries about the Penates of Lavinium, described the ritual of the October horse in the Campus Martius, attributed the introduction of coinage to Servius Tullius, etc. He obviously had a detailed account of the origins of Rome. I see no reason to doubt that Lycophron wrote his *Alexandra* about 270 B.C., after having read some Timaeus. If this is so, lines 1226–31 must be interpreted as a recognition of the new situation through a traditional formula: Rome by now rules land and sea. But if anybody refuses to believe that about 270 B.C. Lycophron could say about the Romans: 'And the fame of the race of my ancestors shall thereafter be exalted to the highest by their descendants who shall with their spears win the foremost crown of glory, obtaining the sceptre and monarchy of earth and sea' (transl. A. W. Mair, Loeb

Library), we shall not quarrel about the date of the *Alexan-dra*. Enough has been written about it. There are other signs that the Greeks began to notice the peculiarities of Roman social life and of Roman behaviour in international affairs. True enough, the famous set of Roman values – *fides, con-stantia, severitas, gravitas, dignitas, auctoritas*, etc. etc. – was discovered for the first time by German professors during the First World War, and helped their pupils to mark time while Hitler was deciding what to do with the classics. But a few characteristic Roman features were truly appreciated by the Greeks in the third century B.C.

Roman *fides* found its way into the coins of Locri about 274 B.C. (B. V. Head, *Historia Numorum*², 104); the *devotio* of Decius at Sentinum apparently attracted the attention of the contemporary historian Duris (76 F 56 Jacoby); the exemplary rebuke of a Roman *matrona* to her son was reported by Callimachus in his *Aetia* (fr. 107 Pfeiffer). Eratosthenes admired both the Roman and the Carthaginian political order (Strabo 1.4.9). Aristos of Salamis in Cyprus, who probably lived in the middle of the third century B.C., is said by Arrian (7.15.5) to have been one of the two historians who not only spoke of an embassy of the Romans to Alexan-der the Great, but made Alexander prophesy the future great-ness of Rome, so impressed was he by the envoys. Unfor-tunately the text of Arrian is ambiguous about the authorship of the prophecy. At the end of the century Philip V of Macedon presented the Roman policy concerning citizenship as a model to the reluctant inhabitants of Larissa (*Syll.*³ 543). These are stock examples, but they go to show that the Greeks, however vaguely, were discovering in Rome some-thing they did not possess themselves.

It is pleasant to contemplate the Fabii learning Greek, while the Greeks were admiring Roman *fides*. But we ought perhaps to give more attention to another fact. The decisive period of the assimilation of Greek culture in Rome is that of the first two Punic Wars. While fighting against Carthage, the Romans learnt Greek and absorbed Greek customs and knowledge at increasing speed. There was no corresponding increase in the Greek interest in Rome. One may even detect a waning of attention to Roman peculiarities. Now that the conquerors of Pyrrhus were involved in an apparently endless struggle with Carthage, the Romans seemed to recede from the horizon of the Greek intellectuals. Between the subtle observations of the period of about 270–240 and the adulation of poems like that by Melinno – which, though undated, places itself naturally in the early second century – we have to recognize a gap. But 240–200 B.C. were exactly the years in which Greek epics, tragedy, comedy and historiography became part of the Roman way of life. Why the Romans threw themselves into the difficult business of absorbing the culture of one foreign nation just when they were involved in exhausting wars with another foreign nation, remains one of those puzzles which characterize nations in their most inscrutable and decisive hours. No doubt collaboration with the Greek or Hellenized aristocracies of southern Italy and Sicily had become essential to Rome. But this is not a sufficient explanation. The assimilation of Greek language, manners and beliefs is indistinguishable from the creation of a national literature which, with all the imitation of alien models, was immediately original, self-assured and aggressive. There could hardly be a more irrepressible pair of characters than Naevius and Cato, the creators respectively of Roman national epic and drama and of Latin literary prose. The creation of this literature in Latin involved men whose native language was either certainly or probably not Latin: Livius Andronicus' first language was Greek; Ennius had Oscan; Naevius, being a Campanian, probably also spoke Oscan as a child; Plautus must have been brought up on Umbrian, and Terence apparently started with Punic. The comedy-writer Statius Caecilius was a Celtic speaker by birth, an Insuber from northern Italy (St Jerome, *Chron.* a. 1838, p. 138 Helm), and apparently the first writer the proud city of Milan ever produced. I would be more cautious about M. Pacuvius, the writer of tragedies, a relative of Ennius. He came from

17

Brundisium, the place where the most famous Messapic inscription was found (Whatmough no. 474), but Brundisium
became a Latin colony in 244 B.C. and had long-standing
connections with Greek Tarentum, to which Pacuvius ultimately retired. He may have spoken only Greek and Latin.

It was left to the Roman aristocrats to write in Greek –
either in historical works or in formal speeches. Not by
chance. The Romans had an old tradition of chronicling
which was kept in the hands of aristocratic pontiffs. Only a
Roman aristocrat – perhaps himself a pontiff – such as Fabius
Pictor could break this tradition and make the native version
of Roman history available to the educated world at large, as
the natives of other countries were doing. It was by writing
history in Greek that Fabius Pictor revolutionized history
in Rome; we need not be surprised that he also used Greek
sources when they were available, such as Diocles of Pepare-
thus on Romulus (Plut. *Rom.* 3, 8). Making public speeches
in Greek was more daring. There is evidence that the
Romans duly made fools of themselves in front of sophisti-
cated Greek audiences. L. Postumius Megellus' bad Greek
produced hilarity in Tarentum in 282 B.C. and contributed to
the subsequent war (Dionys. Hal. 19.5; Appian. *Samn.* 7).
But slowly a capital difference between Romans and Greeks
emerged. The Romans spoke Greek to the Greeks. Flamininus (Plut. *Flam.* 6), the father of the Gracchi (Cic. *Brutus*
20.79), and Lutatius Catulus (Cic. *De orat.* 2.7.28) were fine
Greek speakers. That paragon of an intolerable and un-
fortunate proconsul, P. Licinius Crassus Dives Mucianus,
consul 131, could reply in five different dialects to Greek
petitioners (Val. Max. 8.7.6; Quint. *Inst. Orat.* 11.2.50). It
was for the Roman to decide whether he would speak in
Latin or in Greek to a Greek public – that is, with or without
interpreter – and Aemilius Paulus could skilfully pass from
one language to the other (Liv. 45.8.8; 29.3). Only in the
case of Cato may we suspect that he had no alternative to
speaking in Latin, though Plutarch is convinced that he could
have spoken Greek, if he had wanted to (Plut. *Cat.* 12).

The Greeks, as far as I know, never had a choice. They could only speak Greek to the Romans, and it was for the Romans to decide whether they wanted an interpreter. We must assume that in 280 B.C. Cineas spoke Greek in the Roman Senate and was translated by an interpreter (Plut. *Pyrrh.* 18). An interpreter is specifically mentioned for the mission of the three philosophers on behalf of Athens in 155 B.C.: the interpreter was one of the senators, C. Acilius (Aul. Gell. *N.A.* 6.14.9; Macr. *Sat.* 1.5.16). Apollonius Molon was heard in the Roman Senate without the help of an interpreter in the time of Sulla (Val. Max. 2.2.3).

With such easy-going absorption of Greek culture, there was no particular difficulty in adorning one's family with Greek ancestry in competition with the better established Trojan families. The tradition of an Arcadian settlement in Latium was accepted by Fabius Pictor at the end of the third century B.C. (fr. 1 Peter). Euander was supposed to have introduced a Greek dialect into Latium which, duly corrupted, became Latin (Varro fr. 295 Funaioli; Dion. Hal. 1.90.1). The Sabines looked like modern, austere Lacedaemonians. They acquired Spartan ancestry (Dion. Hal. 2.49; Plut. *Num.* 1.1). According to Servius, Cato *ipse* told the story that the Laconian Sabus, a contemporary of Lycurgus, migrated to Latium (fr. 51–2 P.). The Sabine Claudii naturally became the patrons of their Spartan relatives (Suet. *Tib.* 6.2; cf. Dio 54.7.2; Silius Italicus 8.412). The Fabii answered by claiming descent from Hercules. The earliest evidence known to me about the special devotion of the Fabii to Hercules goes back to Fabius Cunctator in the second Punic War (Plin. *N.H.* 34.40). It is virtually certain that Friedrich Muenzer was mistaken in taking the Herculean legend of the Fabii as an invention of an Augustan antiquarian (P.–W., s.v. Fabii). It is, however, true that Roman aristocrats were usually wary of divine origins. Greek or Trojan ancestors were quite enough to support their claims to power.

I have of course no intention of suggesting that this intellectual and, by implication, political revolution went on without a single hitch. Epicurean philosophers were thrown out of Rome either in 173 or in 154 B.C. (Athen. 12.547a). In 161 there was a *senatus consultum* prohibiting the residence in Rome of philosophers and rhetoricians (Sueton. *De gramm. et rhetor.* 25 Brugnoli; cf. Aul. Gell. *N.A.* 15.11.1). The contradictory attitudes of Cato are in no need of further illustration. Cato knew Hellenistic historiographical, agricultural and military theory probably better than any of his Latin contemporaries, but indulged in mock fury against Greek writers and especially against Greek doctors: 'iurarunt inter se barbaros necare omnes medicina' (Plin. *N.H.* 29.14). A generation earlier Naevius had been silenced after a conflict with the aristocratic Metelli. He was first jailed and then compelled to leave Rome; he is said to have died in the Punic city of Utica, a remarkable place to go for a disgraced Roman intellectual (St Jerome, *Chron.* a. 1816, p. 135 Helm). The details are too uncertain for any useful discussion, but the meaning of the episode is that about 200 B.C. one Roman writer had deluded himself about his chances of importing fifth-century Athenian freedom of speech into Rome (Cic. *Verr.* Actio prima, 1.10.29 and Ps.-Asconius *ad. l.* p. 215 Stangl). Greek and Roman intellectuals had to learn that in Rome Hellenization implied respect for the ruling order. The majority of writers complied and were rewarded. The ex-Greek slave, Livius Andronicus, attained to respectability and influence; he was allowed to have his own 'collegium', a coveted privilege (Festus p. 333 M.= 446 L.). Ennius was imported into Rome from Sardinia by Cato: a piece of information (Corn. Nep. *Cato* 1.4) Professor E. Badian does not seem to me to have invalidated (*Ennius*, Fondation Hardt *Entretiens* XVII (1972), 155–6). Cicero depicted Ennius as a friend of the Scipios (Cic. *Pro Arch.* 9.22) and of the Fulvii Nobiliores (*Tusc. Disp.* 1.3; *Brutus* 79). Terence lived in close familiarity with Scipio Aemilianus and C. Laelius. From the prologues to the *Heautontimorumenos* and the *Adelphoe* we know that his competitors had tried to discredit him for this. Polybius of course, a hostage in Rome since 167, entered the same circle under similar conditions of clientship.

Seen as a whole the assimilation of Greek culture and language was easy and quick. Greek philosophers and rhetoricians became part of the Roman establishment. When in 92 B.C. somebody tried to establish a school of eloquence in Latin – presumably to serve some *popularis* cause – the censors of the day were firmly against it; they declared themselves in favour of Greek, as against Latin, rhetoric (Suet. *De gramm. et rhetor.* 25; Cic. *De orat.* 3.24.93). As one might expect, teachers of Latin eloquence, too, soon became respectable. But Cicero told one of his correspondents that he had been discouraged by his elders and betters from attending such a school: 'continebar autem doctissimorum hominum auctoritate' (Suet. *De rhetor.* 26). Greek became virtually compulsory for the support of the Roman Empire.

We shall never be able to decide how much of the success of Roman imperialism is implicit in this determined effort by the Romans to learn to speak and think in Greek. Nor can we do more than guess at the consequences of the Greek ignorance of Latin. Gaetano Salvemini used to maintain that Mussolini ended in disaster because he always said *Ja* to Hitler at the wrong moment. Being vain, Mussolini did not want to admit that his German was insufficient for a diplomatic conversation. The Greeks at least did not make any attempt to conceal their ignorance of Latin. But did they understand fully how formidable this nation was which could persuade men from Magna Graecia, Campania, Umbria and Africa to use their knowledge of Greek for the creation of a literature in Latin? In the period 160–60 B.C. there were Greeks who studied Roman history and institutions, not to flatter the Romans (as too many did), but to understand Roman conquests. We shall have to ask ourselves in the next lecture to what extent they succeeded with so little Latin at their disposal. Compulsory Greek, we all agree, is indispensable for the upkeep of an empire; but is compulsory Latin necessary to save oneself from an empire?

2

Polybius and Posidonius

How many tear-drops are implied in the simple Greek word ἐδάκρυεν, 'he wept'? Classical scholars can be trusted to ask such questions. The occasion is famous, the protagonists are distinguished; Scipio Aemilianus crying over burning Carthage, Polybius suitably present and ready to elicit the right answer: 'turning round to me at once and grasping my hand, Scipio said: "A glorious moment, Polybius, but I have a dread foreboding that some day the same doom will be pronounced upon my own country"' (38.21.1, transl. W. R. Paton). The mutilated text of the passage of Polybius has come down to us in the *Excerpta de sententiis* and the key-word ἐδάκρυεν, 'he wept', has to be supplied from Diodorus (32.24) with the support of Appian, *Punica* 132: they are known to have used Polybius directly or indirectly. The supplement seems to be right. Scipio did cry, and classical scholars are therefore entitled to ask how many tears he shed. As Professor A. E. Astin observes in his very valuable book on Scipio Aemilianus (1967): 'By ἐδάκρυεν Diodorus (Polybius) need not necessarily mean that Scipio shed a flood of tears, that he truly wept. It is also possible to envisage moist eyes, with a tear or two trickling down either cheek; and this would be much more consistent with Polybius' praise of Scipio's attitude, that of "a great, a perfect man, a man in short worthy to be remembered"' (p. 285).

If classical scholars are entitled to count tears, they should not, however, allow public school prejudices to trouble their

22

historical judgement. Polybius was ready to accept many, many tears from his illustrious friend and protector. He had registered with warm approval the tears of Antiochus III, when the rebel Achaeus was brought to him 'bound hand and foot' (8.20.9). He tells of the Elder Scipio's tears on appreciating the humiliations to which the royal ladies were exposed after his capture of Carthago Nova (10.18.13). Polybius did not invent such situations. It is almost certainly from a Roman source – an autobiographical letter by Scipio Nasica – that Plutarch derived his picture of Aemilius Paulus, the father of Scipio Aemilianus, receiving King Perseus as a prisoner: 'Aemilius saw in him a great man whose fall was due to the resentment of the gods and his own evil fortune, and rose up and came to meet him, accompanied by his friends and with tears in his eyes' (*Aem. Paul.* 26.5–6 transl. B. Perrin). In the report of Plutarch and therefore (as I believe) of Scipio Nasica, this was an occasion for Aemilius Paulus to indulge in a lecture on Fortune. It is here irrelevant to decide whether the Roman generals learnt how to cry from their Hellenistic opposite numbers just as they learnt from them how to write autobiographical letters on their victories. The Romans did not have to wait for the Greeks to discover that they were mortals. In his triumph the victorious general was supposed to be accompanied by a slave repeating to him at suitable intervals: 'Respice post te, hominem te memento' (Tertull. *Apol.* 33.4; Arr. *Diss.* 3.24.85; Zon. 7.21.9); though this, too, may arguably be a Hellenistic intrusion into a Roman ceremonial.

What matters is that Polybius found in Rome people who would not differ from educated Greeks in their interests, ideas and emotional reactions. Some at least of the leading Romans felt and behaved in a way which seemed to him perfectly understandable and eminently sensible. According to his own account, as soon as he was brought to Rome as a hostage in 167 B.C. he became a friend of the two surviving sons of Aemilius Paulus by sharing some books with them. He was then about thirty-five years old, and the younger of these sons, who through being adopted into the *gens Cornelia* had become Publius Cornelius Scipio Aemilianus, the future destroyer of Carthage, was about eighteen years old. When Polybius and Scipio found themselves alone in the neighbourhood of the Forum (Polybius goes on to tell us) Scipio, 'blushing slightly, addressed him in a quiet and gentle way: "Why, Polybius, since there are two of us, do you constantly converse with my brother and address to him all the questions and explanations but ignore *me*?"' (31.23.8–9). An explanation in fact followed, after which Scipio, 'grasping Polybius' right hand in both his own and pressing it warmly, said: "Would I could see the day on which you, regarding nothing else as of higher importance, would devote your attention to me and join your life with mine"' (31.24). It is evident that Polybius self-consciously turned this meeting into a Socratic episode, and Paul Friedländer was reminded of the opening scene of the 'Greater Alcibiades' (*Am. Journ. Phil.* 66 (1945), 337–51 = *Plato* 1 (1958), 322–32). The title of his article, 'Socrates enters Rome', is certainly justified on a wider basis. A century later, Cicero attributed to Scipio Aemilianus and his friends the introduction of Socrates' teaching in Rome. As he says in *De republica* (3.5): 'Scipio and his friends added to the native usage of our ancestors the teaching of Socrates coming from abroad.'

Polybius could not have written his history as he did if he had not found in Rome an aristocracy which he could instinctively understand because he shared its attitude to life. The common basis was provided by the large-scale infiltration of Hellenistic thoughts and customs into Rome during the previous century. But we must allow for a certain amount of give and take. Plutarch reports in the *Quaestiones Conviviales* (IV, Proemium) one of the pieces of advice which Polybius was supposed to have given to Scipio after he took charge of him: 'Never return from the Forum until you have made a new friend of one of your fellow citizens.' This shows that Polybius grasped very early the system of 'amicitiae', that is of clientships, which supported the power of the Roman aristocracy. With equal ease and sympathy he penetrated into that maze of Roman rules, conventions and unexpected reactions in which many other Hellenistic politicians lost their way. In his accounts of Roman men and manners, Polybius is never troubled by difficulties of interpretation. His walks through the streets of Rome must have been accompanied by a constant sensation of *déjà vu*. He gives the impression of recognizing rather than of discovering. He lacks the sense of surprise. He is the prototype of the historian who never marvels, just as Herodotus is the prototype of the historian who always marvels. He had of course his grasp of military and diplomatic practice to help him; and he was firmly convinced that the Roman constitution was open to analysis in Greek terms. He did not claim to be absolutely original in his cyclical theory of constitutional changes. But even if he was more original than he himself claims, he was only producing one of many variations on a Greek scheme. Furthermore, he had an acute sense of deviation from the norm in any society. He praised Scipio Aemilianus' generosity to his relatives by remarking: 'Such conduct would naturally be admired anywhere, but in Rome it was a marvel; for absolutely no one there ever gives away anything to anyone if he can help it' (31.26.9). Interestingly enough, he seems to have been helped in his description of Roman institutions by handbooks available to Roman officers and magistrates.

His description of the Roman military camp (6.27–42) is almost certainly derived from a book, and even the description of a Roman levy on the Capitol (6.19–21) seems to be taken from a written account, since, as Professor Brunt has lately shown in detail, it can hardly have corresponded to contemporary practice (*Italian Manpower 225 B.C.–A.D. 14* (1971), 625–34). We may have to admit that Polybius did not always check his facts even when it would have been easy to do so. In other cases, where he was not present, we know that he was contradicted by contemporary sources. Plutarch noted that he and his contemporary Scipio Nasica disagreed

25

on certain details of the battle of Pydna (*Aem. Paul.* 16.2). Polybius' constant presupposition that the Romans are both transparent in their motives and fundamentally reasonable in their actions involves three assumptions: (1) that the Roman upper class is not divided by internal conflicts of interests and convictions; (2) that it controls the lower classes of Rome, the Latins and the other allies without much difficulty; (3) that its aim of world domination is eminently rational and does not pose many problems. Let me illustrate these three points together very briefly.

We have to go to Livy and to minor sources for evidence of the conflicts inside the Roman ruling class and between Romans and allies in the first half of the second century B.C. Polybius does not seem to have noticed the feuds inside Rome which accompanied what may appear to us the most uncontroversial aspect of the Roman expansion in Liguria and in Piedmont. He does not mention that Scipio Nasica was against the destruction of Carthage because Rome needed a rival in order to keep sober and alert. Doubts have repeatedly been expressed on the authenticity of Nasica's speech in the Roman Senate to support this point of view. Polybius' silence has provided the main ground for this scepticism (W. Hoffmann, in R. Klein, *Das Staatsdenken der Römer* (1966), 224). But Nasica's speech was already known to Diodorus (34.33.4; cf. Plut. *Cato maior* 27.1–2; Appian. *Pun.* 69.315) and consequently to his source in the first century B.C.: its content agrees with an opinion which the source of Appian. *Pun.* 65.298–91 attributed to Scipio Africanus. Polybius' silence may mean nothing more than that he was inclined to ignore the differences of opinion among his Roman protectors. An element of prudence is not to be excluded. He hastened to repeat Cato's jokes even when they were directed against the Greeks – and indeed against Polybius himself (31.25.5; 35.6; 36.14; 39.1). But he does not tell us of the forty-four accusations which were brought against Cato at various times (Plin. *N.H.* 7.100; Plut. *Cato maior* 15.4). Even if we do not want to take too seriously the feuds between Cato and Quinctius Flamininus (Plut. *Cato maior* 17.1; 19.2) and between Cato and the brothers P. and L. Scipio (Plut. *Cato maior* 3.5–6; Nepos *Cat.* 1.3) which are conspicuous in later biographical tradition, it remains true that Polybius is vague enough about the trial of Scipio Africanus to lead a historian like De Sanctis (*St. dei Romani* IV, 1, p. 594) to the false conclusion that Africanus was never tried at all (Polyb. 23.14.). There is nothing in Polybius about the Bacchanalia scandal, nothing about the measures against the Latins, for instance in 187 B.C. (Liv. 39.3). True enough, we have only fragments of his history; but it cannot be by chance that while the Greek side of his tale is full of internal conflicts, the story of Italy is miraculously free of them. Nor is the argument from silence the only one. Perhaps even more significant is what Polybius makes of that anthropologist's delight, the funeral processions in which the Roman aristocrats paraded hirelings masked as their own ancestors. We owe to Polybius the only description of this procession – which shows his flair. It is also undeniable that he sees a part of the truth – such ceremonies educated the young at large to respect their elders and betters and to aspire to the same glory (Polyb. 6.54.3): they were civic festivals. But Polybius entirely overlooks the other aspect – the display of ancestor cult and of family pride, the assertion by certain *gentes* against other *gentes* of their traditional right to rule. By underplaying the internal conflicts within the Roman aristocracy and the tensions between Romans and non-Romans in Italy, Polybius created an atmosphere in which Roman conquests became both easy to understand and difficult to question. I once suggested to a French audience that a book on *Les silences du Colonel Polybe* would be instructive.

I need not here emphasize the point that nobody can expect Polybius to study the dynamics of Roman imperialism. The very word imperialism is modern; I do not know of any serious attempt to grasp the dynamics of any imperialism – old or new – before J. A. Hobson's *Imperialism* in 1902. If

I am wrong, I am wrong in the company of comrade Vladimir Ilyich Ulyanov who took the same view in his book of 1917 on *Imperialism, the Highest Stage of Capitalism*. Even meditations on the military spirit of the Romans such as Montesquieu's *Grandeur des Romains et leur décadence* – though suggested by Polybius – are unthinkable in antiquity. But the ancients gave some attention to the individuals who started wars and to the justice or injustice of their actions: occasionally they went beyond the individuals to discuss the conflicts of interests between states. Herodotus made Atossa advise Xerxes to conquer Greece; Theopompus put the personality of Philip at the beginning of his history of the Macedonian conquest of Greece. Thucydides distinguished himself by transferring the real cause of the Peloponnesian War to the more impersonal fears inspired in the Peloponnesians by Athens. Polybius pursues the search for individual responsibilities where non-Roman kings and leaders are concerned. He names Hannibal, Philip V, Perseus and the Aetolians and the Achaean leaders as being responsible for wars they could have avoided. But with one exception (to which we shall soon return) he does not ask such questions about the Romans. Even the arbitrary occupation of Sardinia by the Romans, though freely admitted to be unjust (3.28.2), is not directly connected with the origins of the second Punic War. While in examining the conduct of Greeks, Carthaginians, Macedonians and Eastern potentates Polybius conforms to the pattern of the majority of the Greek historians, he makes an exception for the Romans. Their impulse to rule is neither analysed nor questioned. What is emphasized in their case is something very different: the support which their political constitution and generally speaking their customs and habits gave them in their drive towards world-rule. This does not exclude negative judgements on Roman individuals who showed themselves inferior to normal standards of prudence or wisdom: even Claudius Marcellus is blamed for his lack of prudence (10.32.7–12). But the Romans are never questioned on their basic policy.

It is evident that Polybius has identified himself with Roman success. He therefore experiences no difficulty in writing a history for both the Greeks and the Romans. He makes it repeatedly clear that he addresses himself to the Greeks who have little knowledge of Roman institutions; but on the other hand he refers to Roman readers (6.11.3–8) and is quite obviously looking at them over his shoulder. He explains to the Greeks why the Romans won, and explains to the Romans the meaning and the conditions of their own victory. But this should not be taken as moral and intellectual capitulation to the Romans. Polybius acts as a Greek who has a vital interest in the proper functioning of the Roman hegemony over Greece. He finds no pleasure in the behaviour of the Romans after the destruction of Corinth and says so (Book 38). Indeed it is evident that the events of 146, both at Carthage and at Corinth, filled him with bitterness and anxiety. Just because he had by now become an important agent of the Roman rule, and one whom the Romans trusted, he felt the need of continuing his history from 166 to 146 to show how the Romans had behaved. It is difficult for us to see what Polybius added to his history after 146, but where the additions are clear the anxiety and the warning are equally clear. Polybius explains in Book 3 why he proposes to extend his exposition to cover the next twenty years by saying: 'Since judgements regarding either victors or vanquished based purely on the actual struggles are not final. . . I must append an account of the subsequent policy of the conquerors and their method of universal rule, as well as of the various opinions and appreciations of their rulers entertained by the rest' (3.4.4–6). When he comes to the destruction of Carthage in 146 he records the contrasting opinions of the Greeks about Rome's conduct (36.9). This was an unusual step for Polybius, the more remarkable because he had taken part in the destruction of Carthage. As he never questioned the basic principles of Roman expansion, we should not waste our time in trying to decide whether or not he approved of the destruction of Carthage. What is new and important is that he should consider it necessary to convey the contrasting opinions of the contemporary Greeks to their Roman masters. He was obviously worried about the future of a state which had to resort to terror in order to maintain its supremacy. As he says in that section of Book 3 which is a later addition, 'No man with any intelligence goes to war with his neighbours simply for the sake of crushing an adversary' (3.4.10). If Diodorus in Book 32 echoes Polybius, we have here further confirmation that Polybius saw Rome entering the stage of 'terror and repression'. It is doubtful whether, given his premises and the situation in which he found himself, he could have done more than convey the expression of widespread discontent and indicate at the same time that something had changed in the Roman governing class.

Polybius paved the way for the other Greek intellectuals who accepted Roman rule and collaborated with it. Their aim was not to discover the roots of Roman imperialism or even to persuade the Greeks that it was acceptable. Their task was to persuade the Roman leaders to behave in a way which would not alienate the majority of their subjects and consequently would not imperil the position of those upper-class provincials who had identified their interests with Roman rule. The Romans had put an end to the social struggles in the Greek cities and had given an implicit guarantee of survival for the wealthy. There were many people in Greece who felt grateful for the repression of even minor social disturbances, such as that of Dyme in Achaia about 116 B.C., so typically described in the letter by the Roman proconsul Quintus Fabius Maximus to the magistrates of the city: abolition of debts and contracts (*SIG*³ 684). But it was essential for the beneficiaries to insist that such a policy should not be stultified by plunder, wanton destruction, reckless deployment of military force and general contempt for the welfare of the provincials. Even relatively unsophisticated observers could see that the Roman leaders were basically interested in their own power and in their own wealth; their estates, the number of their slaves and all the other signs of unilateral exploitation were daily becoming more conspicuous. To Polybius, and later to his continuator Posidonius, the ancient Roman simplicity was reassuring (Polyb. 6.57.5; 31.25; 36.9; Posid. fr. 59 Jacoby). We may suspect that Polybius' contemporary, the Stoic philosopher Panaetius of Rhodes, did not disagree on this. At least we hear from Cicero that Panaetius registered – apparently with approval – the opinion of Scipio Aemilianus that men elated by continuous success should be disciplined like horses after a battle. This is the only quotation from Panaetius (*De officiis* 1.26.90) which can give us some idea of the conversations he had with Scipio in his many years of familiarity with him.

All the contributions to the theory of Roman imperialism which modern scholars have ascribed to Panaetius are of course pure products of the imagination. There is not one fragment of Panaetius dealing with political matters; and what Cicero derived in his *De officiis* from Panaetius' *Peri Kathekontos* (Cic. *ad Atticum* 16.11.4; *De officiis* 3.2.7–10) has no bearing on conquest or provincial government. Out of this Professor Pohlenz made a whole book with the promising title *Antikes Führertum*. But the fact remains that Panaetius lived for some time in Rome, as the *Index Stoicorum Herculanensis*, an excellent source, states (73); and there seems to be no reason to doubt the statement of Cicero in *Pro Murena* that he was the guest of Scipio (31.56). Furthermore, we have the unimpeachable information of his pupil Posidonius that he was invited by Scipio to be his companion on the diplomatic journey to the East about 140 B.C. (fr. 30 Jacoby). The passage of Cicero's *De officiis* with which we are concerned gives some indication of the area of agreement between the Roman leader and his helpful philosopher client. They both thought that too much success and power represented a danger. The context makes it certain that political power was implied. The context makes it also virtually certain that Panaetius derived from Scipio's remark the consequence that the more powerful and successsful a man is, the more he will need the advice of his friends. This was clearly the position in which he wanted to put Scipio in relation to himself. Panaetius' concern, like Polybius', was to encourage those whom he considered both the most influential and the best disposed of the Romans not to abuse their power.

The same attitude is recognizable in the fragments of the histories of Posidonius, the pupil of Panaetius who, amidst all his philosophical work, decided to become the continuator of Polybius for the period after 146 B.C. It is uncertain whether Posidonius concluded his histories with the events of Sulla's dictatorship or whether he extended them to include the Eastern wars of Pompey. But if his history did not go down to 63 B.C. we must assume that he wrote a separate monograph on the wars of Pompey; the difference is not great. Posidonius was active between about 100 and 50 B.C.: in 86 he was an ambassador to Rome and saw Marius. His early acquaintance with Publius Rutilius Rufus at the school of Panaetius must have given him a first taste of Roman *optimates*: later he had Pompey and Cicero among his admirers.

Posidonius provided some sort of theory to justify political power and conquest. He seems to have given a sketch of the evolution of sovereignty from the king of the golden age to his own time (Sen. *Ep.* 90). He did not object, as far as we know, to the permanent dependency of clients and serfs, such as the clients of the Celtic chieftains (frs. 15.17.18 Jacoby) and the serfs of the Greek city of Heraclea Pontica called Mariandyni (fr. 8 Jacoby). He may even have specifically praised the Roman rule over Spain, though the passages from Strabo which are quoted to prove this seem to me simply thoughts of Strabo himself praising the *pax romana* of Augustus. What is, however, essential is that Posidonius was very worried about the social turbulence of his time, even if it did not affect his home island, Rhodes, as seriously as the Greek mainland.

The discontent with Rome had at last resulted in rebellions

of slaves and of the lower classes, indirectly or even directly supported by those who at the two opposite corners of the Roman Empire were trying to defend their own independence, the Spanish tribes and Mithridates, king of Pontus. Polybius' misgivings about the future of Rome had proved justified – and this was perhaps one of the main reasons why Posidonius decided to continue his work. Posidonius considered the chattel-slavery of his time an evil. He thought that the inhabitants of Chios, who according to tradition had introduced slavery into Greece, deserved the punishment of being themselves enslaved, which Mithridates had inflicted on them for quite different reasons (fr. 38 Jacoby). He depicted the life of enslaved mine workers in dark colours, and was altogether sensitive to the suffering of the humble (as Professor Strasburger has reminded us in *Journ. Rom. Stud.* 55 (1965), 40–53). But he was not moved by such feelings to sympathize with the rebels and the subversive. His picture of the democratic tyranny of Athenion, the Aristotelian who led the anti-Roman movement in Athens in 87, is the most hostile image of a popular leader in Greek literature – and I know of few comparable portraits in other literatures (fr. 36 Jacoby). He was equally outspoken about the servile wars in Sicily (as we can deduce from Diodorus who follows him). The question for him was how to avoid the rise of such movements. He was more concerned with prevention than repression; and in any case by the time he wrote it had been shown that repression could be safely left in the hands of the Romans. Prevention meant to Posidonius moderate use of power, responsible treatment of the poor and even of the slaves. He took up in different terms the position of Polybius and Panaetius.

This can be inferred from the line which Diodorus takes in what is left of Books 32–7. I am by no means inclined to consider Diodorus a mere copyist of his sources, and I know only too well that by stylistic criteria one could prove that Sir Ronald Syme is the author of some of the books written by his pupils. But these passages of Diodorus are different from all the rest of Diodorus: the style has a new vitality, the portraits conjure up strange and irrepressible personalities, the political and moral judgements are far more personal than in the previous books. The portrait of the leader of the Sicilian slaves, Eunus, irresistibly reminds us of the Posidonian fragment on Athenion. Indeed, a fragment of the eighth book of Posidonius quoted by Athenaeus 12.59, p. 542b (= fr. 7 Jacoby) is closely similar to Diodorus 34.34. Instructively enough, it gives details about a Sicilian landowner, Damophilus, which we would otherwise have attributed to the Sicilian Diodorus. I think that for once we need feel no qualms in taking Diodorus as a faithful epitomizer of what must have been a compact and careful section of Posidonius on the slave war in Sicily.

If this is correct, it confirms Posidonius' awareness of the desperate situation of the slaves before the rebellion. Diodorus declares bluntly: 'The slaves, distressed by their hardships and frequently outraged and beaten beyond all reason, could not endure their treatment' (34.2.4). Damophilus by his cruel behaviour brought about 'destruction for him and great calamities for his country' (34.35). The sympathy of Diodorus – that is, of Posidonius – stretches so far as to admit that even during the war the slaves spared some of the owners who had been kind to them. The daughter of that cruel Damophilus 'had done all she could to comfort the slaves who were beaten by her parents': so the slaves not only did not touch her but escorted her 'to the home of certain kinsmen in Catana' (34.39). The historian does not extend his sympathy to the leaders. Eunus 'met such an end as befitted his knavery' (34.23). Nor does he condone the lawlessness (or more precisely, 'the frantic and lawless conduct') of the other rebels (36.11). He well sees that the poor among the free men joined the slaves against the rich, so that the whole social structure was in danger (36.11). Plunder and lawlessness from the free-born slowly emerge as the greater menace. The slave wars are not to be separated, in Posidonius' mind, from the civil wars he had seen in his own time. The

34

opposition of Scipio Nasica to the destruction of Carthage figures so prominently in this account by Diodorus – and therefore by Posidonius – because he was thought to have foreseen the possibility of civil war in Rome if Carthage were to be eliminated: 'but once the rival city was destroyed, it was only too evident that there would be civil war at home and that hatred for the governing power would spring up among all the allies because of the rapacity and lawlessness to which the Roman magistrates would subject them' (34.33.5 transl. F. R. Walton, Loeb). Scipio Nasica was supposed to have almost prophesied not only the Gracchan agitation but also the Social War between Rome and her Italian allies. Posidonius had of course no sympathy for the Gracchi. In Diodorus' account Gaius Gracchus 'made the inferior element in the state supreme over their betters...and from these practices came fatal lawlessness and the overthrow of the state' (34.25). That the Romans had 'abandoned the disciplined, frugal and stern manner of life that had brought them to such greatness, and fell into the pernicious pursuit of luxury and licence' (37.2.1) was, in the same perspective, seen as the primary cause of the Social War. The lesson to be derived was one of moderation: 'Not only in the exercise of political power should men of prominence be considerate towards those of low estate, but also in private life they should – if they are sensible – treat their slaves gently. The more power is perverted to cruelty and lawlessness, the more the character of those subject to that power is brutalized to the point of senselessness' (34.2.33). The Roman politicians of the post-Gracchan period Posidonius admired were those who had shown moderation and had not yielded to the rapacity of the equestrian class, men like Rutilius Rufus or Lucius Sempronius Asellio, a benefactor of Sicily (Diod. 37.5; 8). For the present Posidonius had little choice: he had to rely on his illustrious friend Pompey.

After the half-century or more of Roman rule which separated Posidonius from Polybius the identification of the interests of the Greek wealthy and educated classes with the survival of the Roman Empire had become self-evident. It was this self-evidence that gave authority and courage to Posidonius to speak out to remind the Roman rulers of their errors and misdeeds. Polybius had spent the greater part of his time explaining to Greeks and Romans why the Romans were bound to win. Only in dealing with the events of 146 B.C. did he move towards the position of a cautious critic of Roman society and its methods of government. Posidonius took the Roman victory for granted and analysed the series of crises through which the Roman state had passed in his own time. Though he was bound to give priority to Italy and to the Hellenistic East in his negative analysis of Roman rule, it did not escape him that the barbarous West was involved in the crisis. He knew that these societies of Gaul and Spain had their own rules and virtues, and he described them with obvious sympathy. We shall have more to say about this later. He was not the man to deny the Romans access to the wealth of the barbarians. Like Polybius, we repeat, he did not question the Roman conquests as such. But he spoke of the Italian traders as exploiters of Spain and Gaul (fr. 116–17) and showed how the native defenders of Numantia valued freedom (Diod. 34.4.1–2).

Thus there is a remarkable coherence in the accounts of Polybius and Posidonius, and the latter was right in claiming to have continued the work of the former. Starting from an implicit acceptance of Roman rule they interpreted it as responsible contemporaries, having regard to the needs and interests of the Greek upper class. They used the technique of research they had inherited from their predecessors. Diplomatic and military history had never been so subtly and competently written before Polybius, and the brilliance of Posidonius' social analysis remained unmatched throughout antiquity.

Yet we are still left with the impression that these two Greeks never quite understood what was really happening in the social organism which had become the guarantee of their own survival. Paradoxically both Polybius and Posido-

nius were the victims of their appreciation of Rome. Having
decided that Rome had to be treated as a member of the
civilized community of the Greek world they could not apply
to the study of Roman life those methods which they used,
very competently, to describe barbarians. There was no
attempt to see Rome, as it were, from a distance – as something strange, mysterious in language and religion, frightful
in rituals and formidable in warfare. If Polybius had treated
Rome in the same way as according to a fragment of Book
34 he seems to have treated Alexandria, we would have
gained in understanding. That surviving half-page on Alexandria with its three classes of people is memorable: the
Egyptians, 'an acute and civilized race'; the mercenaries, 'a
numerous, rough and uncultivated set'; and the Alexan-
drians themselves, 'a people not genuinely civilized...but
still superior to the mercenaries for though they are mongrels
they came from a Greek stock and have not forgotten Greek
customs' (34.14). Polybius concludes with a Homeric line
which he would never have used for Rome, however suitable
the adaptation might have been: 'To Egypt is a long and
dangerous road' (*Odys.* 4.483). For the same reasons we
must regret that Posidonius did not try out on Rome that
ethnographical style which makes his Celts live for ever – a
model to the French nation for any past and future extravagance. Neither Polybius nor Posidonius gives any serious
thought even to the phenomenon which had changed the
shape of their own lives: the Hellenization of Italian culture.
True enough, they occasionally notice knowledge of Greek,
adoption of Greek customs, and sympathy for Greek ideas in
individual Romans. But this happens far less systematically
than one would expect. The characterizations of Titus
Flamininus and Aemilius Paulus we have in Polybius
(18.12.3–5; 31.22.1–4) do not emphasize their Hellenization. In Posidonius there seems to have been an excursus in
honour of M. Claudius Marcellus, the hero of the second
Punic War. The reason for this excursus is obscure; it
may be due to the protection accorded to Posidonius by

some descendant of Marcellus. Marcellus is presented as
the model of the old Roman, and his philhellenism is
mentioned only as a political attitude (fr. 43 Jacoby).
Neither Polybius nor Posidonius shows any interest in the
rise of a literature in the Latin language which was rivalling
the Greek. We would not know from Polybius that he was
a contemporary of Ennius, Plautus and Terentius. Posidonius
shows no awareness of living after Accius and Lucilius and
of being the contemporary of Varro – indeed, strictly speaking, he is not even aware of the potentialities of his pupil
Cicero in the world of the mind. Neither of them seems to
have read any work of Latin poetry, though at least Polybius
must have become fluent in the language: even their direct
use of Latin historians is doubtful. What Polybius has in
common with Cato, especially about the Roman constitution,
does not necessarily imply that he read Cato. Indeed, Polybius appears to have gone a step further. He was positively
annoyed at the exhibition of knowledge of the Greek language and customs among his Latin contemporaries. He
censures the younger generation of Romans which, during
the war with Perseus, had been infected by Greek laxity in
social customs (31.25.4), and joins company with Marcus
Porcius Cato, of all people, to ridicule Aulus Postumius for
his untimely display of fluency in Greek (39.1). There may
have been good reasons of prudence in all this. Polybius
himself gives a hint when he says that Aulus Postumius
'made Greek culture offensive in the eyes of the older and
more distinguished Romans'. The result was, however, that
the most important change in Roman life was observed only
at a superficial level. Neither Polybius nor Posidonius realized
what superiority the Roman leaders acquired by the mere
fact of being able to speak Greek, and to think in Greek,
while the Greek leaders needed interpreters to understand
Latin. Even in purely political terms it never seems to have
occurred to Polybius and Posidonius that the command of
a foreign language meant power to the Romans. They were
looking to the old Roman virtues for the explanation of

Roman success, but the Romans had acquired power by divesting themselves of their old Roman habits. A corollary is the absence of any comment on the substitution of Latin for Greek as the leading cultural language in the rest of Italy and on the diffusion of Latin in the western provinces – which at least in the time of Posidonius must have been evident. *If* the long and complex passage of Athenaeus 6 (273a–275b), which Felix Jacoby gives as fragment 59, can be considered a trustworthy summary of Posidonius' views about Roman civilization, two features emerge: (*a*) the Romans preserved for a long time their extreme simplicity of life; (*b*) in that long period they learnt many techniques from various foreigners (Greeks, Etruscans, Samnites and Iberians) and their constitutional principles from the Spartans. Greek literature and philosophy are not mentioned. The presentation of Pompey as a philhellene, as far as we know, was a whim of his agent and panegyrist Theophanes of Mitylene, not of Posidonius.

The reluctance of Polybius and Posidonius to examine the forms of the Hellenization of Rome was a symptom of their uneasy position in their own civilization. The Hellenism that was arriving in Rome included many of those features which men of their aristocratic disposition found distasteful at home. As the Gracchan movement showed, there were still Greek thinkers who encouraged social reform: Blossius of Cumae was one of them. Roman comedy and satire may seem tame to us; one wonders what it looked like in the eyes of Greek aristocrats. Religion was the greatest difficulty: the thin crust of philosophic theism was hardly capable of containing the wilder emotions of prophecy, ecstasy, mystery and ritual cruelty. Eratosthenes reported with obvious sympathy that Arsinoe III Philopator was hostile to the crowd celebrating one of the Dionysiac festivals dear to her husband Ptolemy IV Philopator (241 F 16 Jacoby). Polybius again went a step further by passing over in silence the Roman Bacchanalia which chronologically and typologically can hardly be separated from the new popularity of Dionysus in

Egypt about 210 B.C. He was also silent about the religious
crisis in Rome during the second Punic War: we do not hear
from him about the human sacrifices of that time. He did his
best to turn Scipio Africanus into an unscrupulous manipula-
tor of religious customs he did not share.

Posidonius has the reputation, to a certain extent justified,
of being a religious soul. But he does not seem to have noticed
that Sulla and his friend Pompey were heading for self-
deification: death spared him the task of having to account
for the apotheosis of Caesar. Posidonius found mystical pos-
tures and bogus oracles among the supporters of the slave-
king Eunus and of the barbarous Mithridates. He therefore
lends some support to that candid Italian scholar of unimpeachable erudition, Aurelio Peretti, who, in the year
1942, tried to persuade himself (and if possible his readers)
that no man of Indo-Germanic blood could have protested
against Rome: only Jews and other Orientals scribbled
Sibylline oracles against the ruling power (*La Sibilla Babilonese*, 1943). In fact the first evidence for such oracles comes
from the Peripatetic philosopher and historian Antisthenes
of Rhodes, the contemporary of Polybius. A long fragment of
his history of the years 190–188 B.C. is preserved by Phlegon
of Tralles, the freedman and secretary of Hadrian (257, fr.
36 Jacoby). It tells a remarkable story. About 189 B.C. the
Roman general Publius became mad in the panhellenic sanctuary of Naupactus and began to utter oracles in good Greek
about the end of Roman rule: a king would come from Asia
to take revenge for what the Romans had done to the Greeks.
General Publius announced to his soldiers that they would
soon get proof of the truthfulness of his prophecies: a red
wolf would come and eat him up. Sure enough, the wolf
came and devoured him; only his skull was left which went
on reiterating the prophecy of doom for Rome. Publius was
obviously meant to be Publius Scipio Africanus, who at that
time was operating with his brother in the East. The king
from Asia was probably Hannibal, still living in Asia, if not
Antiochus III himself. The wolf and even the skull (remind-

ing one of the skull which was said to have given its name
to the Capitol) are good Roman elements.

Hannibal was also the object of some sort of pseudo-
historical tale of which a papyrus has preserved a piece that
as far as I know has never been connected with the oracle
transmitted by Antisthenes. The papyrus (*P. Hamburg* no.
129) contains a letter allegedly sent by Hannibal to the
Athenians to announce the victory of Cannae: the forgery is
evident, and its date may well be about 185 B.C. (E. Candiloro, *Studi Class. Orient.* 14 (1965), 171). What is equally
worth noticing is that Antisthenes of Rhodes was one of the
historians Polybius disliked and attacked. Polybius does not
utter one word about the anti-Roman oracles Antisthenes had
so fully reported. Religion was not the area of civilization
which Polybius and Posidonius found easiest to understand.
It was better to talk politics.

But here again an obstacle presented itself which proved
to be insuperable for both Polybius and Posidonius, though
possibly for different reasons. Polybius never quite grasped
the political organization of Italy in his own time. He registered some aspects of it – for instance the separate arrange-
ments for the allied units in the Roman army (6.21.4). But
he does not seem to have tried to give a description of the
Roman system of *municipia* and *coloniae*, Latin allies and
other confederates. Posidonius is less easy to fault, given the
scant numbers of fragments. But if Posidonius had paid
attention to the structure of Italy before or after the Social
War we should know it from Strabo who used his work extensively. Let us, however, confine our attention for a while
to Polybius who was a specialist in constitutional and military
history and who for four centuries conditioned modern
thinking about Republican Rome.

Like the majority of Greek historians Polybius knew that
the army of a state was an element of its constitution. Thus he
took pains to describe the organization of the Roman army
in an excursus in his Book 6 about the Roman constitution.
But he also followed the normal practice of Greek historians

in treating an army at war as something independent of the political organization which had created it. This was quite sensible in the ordinary circumstances of Greek life. Success in war would depend on the ability of the generals, the courage of the troops, the nature of the battlefield, the numbers of the enemy and many other transient factors. Though everybody knew that the constitution of Sparta was behind the reputation of Spartan generals and soldiers, it would have been beneath the ordinary standards of Greek historical judgement to explain an individual victory or defeat as a product of the Spartan constitution. It follows that Polybius as a historian of specific wars was more interested in their conduct than in their institutional background. Naturally he would stress the difference between phalanx and legion in a war between Macedonians and Romans (18.28), but he would not present the war as a conflict between Macedonian monarchy and the Roman mixed constitution. However, what was a healthy attitude in Greek conditions turned out to be dangerous on foreign ground. Polybius was deprived of his only chance of verifying his interpretation of the Roman constitution. If he had had to correlate the conduct of the second Punic War with the decentralization of the Roman state – with its *municipia* and *coloniae* – and with the ever-changing pattern of the Italian alliances, he would soon have discovered that his idea of a mixed constitution in Rome was almost a fiction. The reality was the allegiance to Rome of the local aristocracies which in turn conditioned the behaviour of their clients and followers. Polybius analysed that part of the Roman government which had superficial similarities with a Greek league, but never asked himself how central and southern Italy worked together with the Roman authorities. It is characteristic of him that he transmitted to us a document which gave the number of the soldiers in the Roman army about 225 B.C. and added the number of the men of military age but not under arms: the document distinguished between Roman citizens and allies, and gave specific figures for the main groups of allies (2.23–4). Polybius did not discover this document in an archive: he found it, in all probability, in his Roman predecessor Fabius Pictor who wrote history in Greek in the last decade of the third century (cf. Eutrop. 3.5; Oros. 4.13.6). Polybius gives his reasons for reporting the figures: 'so that it may appear from actual facts what a great power it was that Hannibal ventured to attack, and how mighty was that empire boldly confronting which he came so near his purpose as to bring great disasters on Rome' (2.24.1). More precisely he points out that while 'the total number of Romans and allies able to bear arms was more than seven hundred thousand foot and seventy thousand horse, Hannibal invaded Italy with an army of less than twenty thousand men' (2.24.16–17). It is evident that the way in which Polybius presents his figures leads to absurdities. The figures of the Roman war potential (which is what men of military age means) ought to have been compared with the Carthaginian war potential, but Polybius never does that. Even the figure of the men actually under arms – which Polybius gives as two hundred and ten thousand for 225 B.C. – can hardly be compared with Hannibal's army unless it is properly analysed. I am of course not concerned here with the reliability of the figures themselves but with their use, or rather non-use, by Polybius. There were limits to the concentration of troops because of transportation, food supplies, and manoeuvring on the battlefield which must have been intuitively evident to any ancient general. A hundred thousand soldiers seems to have been the maximum any Hellenistic state was able to gather together for a decisive battle. Antigonus Monophthalmus had ninety thousand soldiers at Ipsus in 301 B.C.; the Seleucid and the Ptolemaic army each consisted of about seventy thousand soldiers at Raphia in 217 B.C. The Roman superiority lay in the capacity for replacement – that is, in the capacity for surviving defeat in one or more battles, as the war against Pyrrhus and the second Punic War amply proved. In its turn this superiority posed problems of collaboration with the allies – and indeed of the balance of forces between

Romans and allies – which occasionally emerge from our sources (for instance, Livy, 25.33.6), but which no ancient writer analysed, not even Polybius.

A description of the precise relations between Rome and her Italian allies (not to speak of the relations between the city of Rome and the periphery of Roman territory proper) would not have been inconceivable in a Hellenistic historian. The ordinary methods of Hellenistic ethnography would have been sufficient. But Polybius would of course have had to jettison his pet idea of the mixed constitution, and generally speaking he would have had to admit that those Romans whose minds appeared so transparent to him were in fact much more mysterious creatures. We may suspect that if Polybius had done his job properly modern scholars would have had less difficulty in finding a way into the Roman mind. We would consequently have to register some losses: we should be deprived of the 490 pages of Kurt von Fritz, *The Theory of the Mixed Constitution in Antiquity* (1954), which would be a pity because, against all probabilities, there is much incidental wisdom and knowledge in this preposterous attempt to compare the surely non-existent mixed constitution of Rome with the doubtfully existent mixed consitution of the United States. We should also have to do without *Rome, la Grèce et les monarchies hellénistiques* by Maurice Holleaux (Paris, 1921), who spent so much intelligence and acumen in trying to make sense of Polybius through the hypothesis that Rome blundered into empire by overrating the aggressive intentions of the Hellenistic states. We may even suspect – and that would be the greatest pity of all – that we should be spared the severe reprimands of Professor Badian for all our sins of omission and commission in not giving proper attention to the difference between conquering Gaul and subjugating Greece.

In other words, even a simple, static analysis of the Roman state in its relation to its allies would have helped us to formulate in more reasonable terms the modern, un-Polybian, problem of Roman imperialism. The dual organization of the

Roman army reflected of course the dual organization of the Roman state. There were on the one side the Roman citizens who (leaving out for our purpose the distinction between *cives cum suffragio* and *cives sine suffragio*) filled the legions. On the other side the conquered enemies under the name of *socii* were compelled to supply troops and to follow Rome into war, but did not pay tribute. Each side had to be kept reasonably satisfied. Long military service could easily become disastrous to the ordinary Roman peasant. But the Roman citizen could be expected to react automatically against enemy action and was entitled to share whatever advantage and glory victory would bring. Even in the second century B.C., when the situation of the Roman peasant-soldier became a political problem, the loyalty of the legions was usually not in question. The *socii* were another matter. They could not be expected to be automatically loyal. Yet they were necessary. They had to be kept busy by war, because otherwise the whole building of the Roman organization would collapse. As military obligations were the only visible tie between Rome and the allies, Rome had to make the most of these obligations lest they became meaningless or, worse, lest the allied armies turn against Rome. Just as the organization of the Athenian empire had its own logic – more tribute and less military partnership – so the organization of the Italian alliance had its own logic – no tribute and therefore maximum military partnership. The loyalty of the allies had to be controlled and encouraged. The control was exercised at two levels, directly through Roman officers, indirectly through the ruling class of the allies themselves: therefore this ruling class had to be supported and even reinforced. But ultimately the ordinary allied soldier had to find some reward for his exertions. The allies had to be given opportunities for glory, booty, settlements and trade in conquered lands. Rome clearly never found a perfect solution for this problem: eventually she had to face the rebellion of the *socii* and grant them entry into Roman citizenship. But the machine worked for about two centuries, from about 280 to 100 B.C.: and the way it worked was that Rome passed from war to war without giving much thought to the very metaphysical question of whether the wars were meant to gain power for Rome or to keep the allies busy. Wars were the very essence of the Roman organization. The battle of Sentinum was the natural prelude to the battle of Pydna – or even to the destruction of Corinth and the Social War.

Polybius' inability to create an appropriate model for the rule of Rome over Italy was inherited by Posidonius and, as far as I know, never remedied by any Greek author. Dionysius of Halicarnassus, who was interested in Italian history as a whole, confined his study to archaic Rome where the problem did not arise. Velleius Paterculus and the Latin source of the first books of Appian's *Civil War* (for which Emilio Gabba suggested the name of Asinius Pollio) came nearer to an Italian version of Roman political history, but by the time they wrote the imperialism of the Republic had turned into the bureaucratic Empire of the Caesars: what these historians said could no longer bear fruit. Polybius and Posidonius remained the masters in the field: the former survived in sufficient measure to impose his interpretation on modern historians, whereas Posidonius reached the Renaissance only through mediators, such as Diodorus and Strabo and perhaps Sallust and Plutarch. Whereas Polybius' fortunes can easily be followed, Posidonius' place in modern thought will be established only when we have a proper study of early ethnography.

From its rediscovery in the early fifteenth century Polybius' history was taken in turn to be a treatise on constitutional forms, a handbook for army officers and a guide for politicians, especially diplomats. From Machiavelli down to Montesquieu, Polybius was the theorist of the mixed constitution. More interestingly, he contributed to the formation of professional armies in the late Renaissance. Justus Lipsius was the classical scholar who introduced him into the military sphere. Maurice of Orange-Nassau and other reformers used Justus Lipsius' *De militia Romana* (1595) with the original text of Polybius as a textbook for educated officers. As early as 1568 the translation of the first book of Polybius by Christopher Watson of St John's College, Cambridge, was preceded by a poem in honour of the historian:

> Polybius reede
> where as in deede
> good physike shoult thou finde.

But it was Casaubon who fifty years later imposed Polybius as the expert in political life, as a far better guide than the fashionable Tacitus. His argument was that Tacitus had chosen the wrong period and provided bad examples for princes, whereas Polybius introduced the modern politicians to a noble period of ancient history. If Casaubon had in mind something more precise than an alternative to the disguised Machiavellianism of the contemporary Tacitists, he did not make it clear. After Casaubon Polybius is to be found in many bypaths of European political life. For instance, Polybius was used in England about 1740 to support the cause of yearly parliaments. Edward Spelman, the translator of Dionysius of Halicarnassus, was apparently the author of the pamphlet published anonymously in 1743 with the title 'A fragment of the sixth book of Polybius...to which is prefixed a preface, wherein the system of Polybius is applied to the government of England.' As I happened to discover casually (not a great discovery), the same pamphlet was given a new frontispiece and a new title in 1747. The new title was even more grandiloquent: 'A Parallel between the Roman and British Constitution; comprehending Polybius's Curious Discourse of the Roman Senate... the whole calculated to restore the true spirit of liberty and to explode dependancy and corruption. Addressed to the young members of the present Parliament.' Even this second edition fails to make it clear to at least one twentieth-century reader why Polybius should be relevant to the cause of one-year parliaments. But the discussion on Polybius provoked by these pamphlets went on at intervals at least until 1783. I ought perhaps to add that

Edward Spelman was the man who said: 'Good God, doth any fellow of a College know anything of Greek.'

It is true that the problem of the balance of power between social classes and organs represented a more vital problem in modern Europe than it had done in Polybius' Rome. Much of the reputation of Polybius as an interpreter of the Roman constitution is a reflection of his authority among modern political thinkers since Machiavelli. It did not of course escape Mommsen that there can hardly be a more foolish political speculation, 'eine thörichtere politische Spekulation', than to represent the Roman constitution as a mixed constitution and to derive from it the success of Rome (*Röm. Geschichte*, 7 ed., II, p. 452). It was Mommsen again who said that Polybius in the treatment of all the questions which concerned law, honour and religion was not only banal but also entirely false, 'nicht bloss platt, sondern auch gründlich falsch'. In their understandable anxiety to save what could be saved of Greek life by co-operating with the Romans, Polybius and, we must add, Posidonius, had left unexplored the most solid substructures of the Roman–Italian complex. What they saw was important enough: the ethos of the Roman leading class, the methods of conquering and ruling, the technicalities of political and military organization. Furthermore, they were intimately acquainted with the Greek republics and Macedonian monarchies of their time, and realistically assessed their capacities to stand up against the Romans. That was enough to make them agents, not only historians, of the Roman expansion. They never asked a question about the justice of Roman rule nor about the real sources of her power. It is perhaps less obvious why both of them – Polybius and Posidonius – should have played such a conspicuous part in exploring the barbarian West and in making it more easily accessible to the Romans. By singling out the Romans as the nation with which the Greeks had the greatest natural affinity, they pushed Celts and Carthaginians into a different category. This was the category of the barbarians, and Greek scholars were traditionally famous for

exploring barbarian lands and making them intelligible to
the civilized. So it happened that both Polybius and Posidonius were involved in exploring the lands of the West, and
more conspicuously the lands of France and Spain – with the
consequences which I hope to illustrate in my next lecture.

Meanwhile, my thought for today is: 'If you want to
understand Greece under the Romans, read Polybius and
whatever you may believe to be Posidonius; if you want to
understand Rome ruling Greece, read Plautus, Cato – and
Mommsen.'

3

The Celts and the Greeks

I

You must not tell a citizen of Marseilles that Petronius, the author of the *Satyricon*, was not born near the Vieux-Port. Sidonius Apollinaris' lines

> et te Massiliensium per hortos
> sacri stipitis, Arbiter, colonum   (*Carmen* 23.155–6)

'You, Petronius, who in the gardens of Marseilles were the worshipper of the sacred tree-stock' are given as evidence for the Massaliote origins of Petronius. They simply prove, as was seen long ago by Conrad Cichorius (*Römische Studien*, 438–42), that an episode in the lost parts of the *Satyricon* was located in Massalia.

But Marseilles could do with another writer. Between Salvian in the fifth century A.D. and our friend Henri-Irénée Marrou in the twentieth century very few names of French intellectuals can be connected with Marseilles. Even now the men who gesticulate along La Canebière look towards the sea rather than towards France. The strong tradition of autonomy which goes back to 600 B.C. survived the guns of Louis XIV and turned a marching song composed at Strasbourg into La Marseillaise.

My tale for today takes us back to the origins of the resistance of Marseilles to the seductions of the Celtic mainland.

II

The epic story of how the citizens of Phocaea abandoned their town rather than submit to the Persians is told by Herodotus 1.163 ff. No story conveys a better impression of the unity of the Mediterranean world in the sixth century B.C. Waves of emotion spread from Asia Minor to Spain as soon as a new protagonist – Persia – disturbed the existing equilibrium of friendships, political alliances and commercial interests. As usual, Delphi had to save its face. Having advised the Phocaeans to settle in Corsica, it had to explain why the enterprise had failed. Some of the Phocaeans had been stoned to death by the Etruscans of Caere, traditional philhellenes; some had to move to Elea in southern Italy. In so far as it justified the oracle, the story of Herodotus was first broadcast from Delphi. But the rest, which starts with the sympathy of Arganthonius, King of Tartessus, for the Phocaeans, was no doubt of Phocaean origin. For it must be admitted that the courageous citizens of Phocaea were among the most consistently self-righteous colonizers of the Greek commonwealth. In founding Lampsacus they killed off all the natives, but they did it in self-defence; the daughter of the local king had warned them of the impending attack. The story was told in detail by a descendant of these settlers, the historian Charon, who, being one of the earliest Greek historians, was in a position to set up a model. The other Phocaean settlement in Ligurian territory at Massalia was described in the same spirit. The story of how the foundation of Massalia was no violent encroachment upon alien territory was already reported by Aristotle (fr. 549 Rose). A Phocaean aristocrat happened to be the guest of the king of the Ligurian tribe of the Segobrigi when the king's daughter was made to choose a husband at a banquet. Needless to say, she chose the Phocaean guest, who became the founder of Massalia on land given to him by his father-in-law. The same story could be read in an expanded and slightly modified form in the *Historiae Philippicae* by Trogus Pompeius, a Celt

who retailed Massaliote traditions and nostalgias at the time
of Augustus. Trogus explains how the idyll between Greeks
and natives came to an end. The Ligurians tried to take
Massalia by surprise during a festival. Duly betrayed by one
of their women, they were punished (43.4). After that the
Massaliotes closed the gates of their city and kept permanent
watch. Here Trogus introduces a note of realism which is
echoed by Livy when he describes how at the beginning of
the second century B.C. a third of the Greeks of Ampurias – a
secondary settlement of the same Phocaeans – manned their
walls every night in fear of the neighbouring Iberians (34.9).
But Trogus soon falls back into imaginary history when he
tells the episode of the chieftain Catumarandus, who had
been persuaded in a dream by a goddess to make peace with
Massalia. Trogus goes on to explain that a little later – that is
about 390 B.C. – the Massaliotes emptied their treasure to
ransom the Romans from the Gauls. I am not the first to
suspect that the inhabitants of Massalia spent their money to
ransom themselves from Catumarandus rather than the
Romans from Brennus. The Phocaeans relied on the help of
their virgin goddess Artemis, but even more on the love of
native princesses – which has seemed un-Hellenic behaviour
to many a modern scholar.

Inevitably, the history of Massalia was one of sharp-eyed
vigilance against her neighbours. It will have been noticed
that the Ligurians, in whose territory the city had been
founded, bore the very Celtic name of Segobrigii. Whatever
the explanation of this fact may be, at least from the late fifth
century B.C. onwards true La Tène Celts watched from their
fortified hills the movements of their Greek neighbours. For
all practical purposes the Massaliotes had to deal with men
who in language, art, tribal customs and, presumably,
Druidic wisdom belonged to the fluid Celtic civilization. It
was altogether a history of successful preservation of traditional political, social and cultural values by a conservative
élite against all odds; even Caesar's move to punish Massalia,
as the ally of Pompey, did not spell disaster. Massalia was cer-

tainly helped in its trade by the other Greek colonies along
the coasts of France and Spain, which, if not by origin, at
least in fact were its own subsidiaries: Nicaea, Antipolis,
Rhode, Emporiae, Mainace, etc. But it is difficult to measure
the effort in military and social co-ordination which such
isolated outposts must have required: they were a liability
just as much as a help.

Massalia poses two problems in relation to the Celtic world.
One is the problem of the contribution of Massalia to the
Hellenization of the Celts. The other is the effect of the
neighbourhood of the Celts on Massalia, and through Massalia on the Greeks in general. The former problem has been
much discussed; the second, though no less curious, is much
less spoken about.

At least in the present stage of research, it would be ridi-
culous to try to isolate the Massaliote component in the
process of penetration of Greek material and spiritual goods
into Celtic territory. This was a territory which at least in the
fourth and third centuries B.C. extended from Spain to the
Black Sea, included northern Italy and large patches of the
Danubian regions, and after 279 B.C. had reached the heart
of Asia Minor – the new Galatia. The points of contact with
the Greek world were innumerable and were increased by the
use of Celts as mercenaries in Italy and practically everywhere
else. In 186 B.C. there were Galatian mercenaries in Egypt
who were able to announce to the world in perfect Greek
from the little temple of Horus in Abydos 'We of the corps
of the Galatians have come and have captured a fox' (Dittenberger, *OGIS* 757). Careful historians, incidentally, warn us
that it could not be a fox, but must have been a jackal.

Even if we confine ourselves for the moment to the late
sixth and fifth centuries B.C., when the options were more
limited, the road of the Rhône was not the only route for
traffic between Celts and Greeks. There were other roads
through the Alps, and other intermediaries: certainly the
Etruscans and probably the Phoenicians, with whom the
Massaliotes had hostile encounters (Thucyd. 1.13.6; Paus.

10.18.7). We do not know whether the Lady of Vix received her gigantic vase – a Laconian one? – through Massalia. Nor do we know whether Massaliote technicians rebuilt in the Greek style the fortress on the Danube at Heuneburg in Württemberg at the end of the sixth century. Only late Gallic coinage imitates Massaliote issues; in the fourth–third centuries B.C. it was distinctly under Macedonian influence. But 'au Pègue', 150 miles north of Massalia, the sixth-century pottery is Ionian – that is, presumably, from Marseilles. At Ensérune the wealth of Greek pottery is hardly to be dissociated from Marseilles. What is more, Celtic and German dialects received very early the Greek verb ἐμφυτεύω in the sense of 'to graft': it has given 'enter' in French, 'impfen' in German, and I like to remember that I first met this word in my childhood as a current term of Piedmontese agriculture. The communication of such a word implies the communication of the technique of grafting and cannot be explained except as a Massaliote loan-word. This brings us near to the suggestion that it was Massalia which provided the Celtic chieftains with a new, more exciting, way of getting drunk at their famous hierarchically organized banquets: wine made mead and beer less prestigious. The Greeks sold wine to the Celts, but also taught them to produce it. It remains true that we do not know when Marseilles became the main receiving point of the tin which was carried on horseback for thirty days from the British Channel. The direct evidence belongs to the first century B.C. (Diod. 5.22.4). But some tin, iron, slaves, hides, wool and gold must have reached Massalia very early, in exchange for wine, oil, salt, bronze and clay vases and mirrors. The spreading of the Greek alphabet among the Celts is again due to Massaliote influence. It may be a development of the third–second centuries B.C. This seems to be the date of Gallic inscriptions in Greek characters. In the first century B.C. Gauls near Massalia wrote their contracts in Greek (Strabo 4.1.5). Caesar found a census of the population in the Greek script when he took over the camp of the Helvetii (*Bell. Gall.*

1.29). We owe to the same Caesar the information that the Druids used the Greek alphabet (6.14).

At least in the Hellenistic age Celts went to Massalia to learn Greek manners and language; this city was a school for the barbarians, according to Strabo (4.1.5; Justin 43.4.1). The suggestion by Justin that the barbarians also learnt something about urbanization is amply confirmed by archaeology, from the Ensérune settlement of the fifth century B.C. to Glanum and the *oppidum* of Entremont in the Hellenistic period. Glanum has become the textbook example of a Celtic settlement according to Greek principles. The human figures found at Entremont indicate that the Celts were at last persuaded to abandon their prejudice against the representation of the human form. And when Caesar mentions six hundred senators among the Nervii (*B.G.* 2.28), it is natural to ask whether the six hundred life senators – *timouchoi* – of Marseilles were their model.

The citizens of Massalia in their turn could not remain insensitive to the surrounding civilization. They used Celtic mercenaries for their own defence, according to Polybius (3.41). They even came to incorporate a small tribe of native neighbours as permanent auxiliary troops; this at least is the information conveyed by Caesar (*B. Civ.* 1.34.4). Varro seems to have stated that in his time Massalia was trilingual, the two foreign languages being of course Latin and Celtic. We would like to have the context of this statement which is transmitted by St Jerome (*In Galat.* 2.426, p. 543 Migne) and Isidore of Seville (15.1.63). At least one Massaliote in the service of the Ptolemies in the second century B.C. has a name, Cinto, probably of Celtic origin (U. Wilcken, *Zeitschr. f. Aegypt. Sprache* 60 (1925), 97). Ancient students of folklore attributed to Celtic influence one of the details of the famous Massaliote hospitality. When friends parted, they exchanged loans of money to be returned in the next life. Being neighbours of the Celts (Valerius Maximus explains), the Massaliotes had learnt from them to believe in the immortality of the soul, a belief not to be despised, as it was shared by the Pythagoreans: 'dicerem stultos, nisi idem bracati sensissent quod palliatus Pythagoras credidit' (2.6.10). Consequently Livy attributes to the consul Cn. Manlius Vulso a speech in 189 B.C. in which, to encourage in the Roman legionaries a contempt for the Galatians, he finds traces of Celtic barbarism even in Massalia: 'Massilia inter Gallos sita, traxit aliquantum ab accolis animorum' (38.17.11). Massalia's prestige among the Celts was high. In 195 B.C. Lampsacus registered the help which her Phocaean sister-city Massalia had given to her, not only at Rome, but also in relations with the Celts of Asiatic Galatia (Dittenberger, *Syll.* 591).

All this evidence only goes to show how easy it would be to build up a completely distorted picture of the life of Massalia in the Hellenistic period. Livy himself, in another context, makes a Rhodian ambassador praise in the Roman Senate the tenacity with which the Massaliotes adhered to Greek traditions, 'ac si medium umbilicum Graeciae incolerent' (37.54.21). The general impression of Massalia in ancient sources is of a city which had decided to remain unchanged in its archaic Hellenic shape. The comparison with Venice is only too obvious; the difference from the Greek colonies of the Black Sea, Olbia, Panticapaeum, etc., is equally obvious. The Massaliotes feared contamination from their neighbours. As Silius Italicus summed up (*Pun.* 15.169–72): 'The settlers from Phocaea, though surrounded by arrogant tribes and kept in awe by the savage rites of their barbarous neighbours, still retain the manners and dress of their ancient home among warlike populations.' Aristotle knows of a time in which the constitution of Massalia had been even more oligarchic than it was in his time (*Pol.* 5.5.2). He recognized that the *plebs* participated to some extent in the affairs of the city (6.4.5). But the constitution was oligarchic enough when Strabo – or his source – described it. Six hundred senators chosen for life ruled the city: they had to be married, to have children and to be sons and grandsons of citizens. We do not know how they were elected; but in practice it can hardly have been more than a co-optation.

There was a smaller executive body of fifteen, and three of these fifteen were apparently the yearly heads of the state. No foreigner was allowed to carry weapons; and no woman was allowed to drink wine (Theophrastus fr. 117 Wimmer = Aelian. *V.H.* 2.38). The morality of public shows was closely controlled. Whoever wanted to commit suicide asked for authorization from the senators; if his reasons were good, he was given his hemlock free of charge. A master who freed a slave could take back his freedom three times in succession; after the third time it was assumed that the judgement of the master could no longer be trusted. This severity of customs was inseparable from the old friendship with Rome. Massalia claimed alliance with Rome from the origins. The friendship was certainly very old, because the Romans deposited in the treasury of the Massaliotes their offering to Delphi after the capture of Veii in 390 B.C. (Diod. 14.93.4; App. *Ital.* 8.11). Common experience of Celtic attacks consolidated the friendship in the fourth century. Towards the end of the third century Hannibal created a new bond between the two cities, as he clearly tried to use the Celts against both. Massalia seemed to the Romans of the late Republic and the early Empire to be a relic of the good old days: 'disciplinae gravitas, prisci moris observantia' (Val. Max. 2.6.7); exactly the place for Agricola to be educated.

So absorbed was Massalia in her effort to remain Greek – and aristocratic – that, to all appearances, she never organized any exploration of the interior of Gaul, and never transmitted any precise knowledge of Celtic institutions and customs to the other Greeks. Here again the difference from the Black Sea colonies which studied the natives and informed Herodotus is obvious. Nobody can doubt that the Massaliotes explored seas and coasts. It was their life. They went round the coasts as far as the Carthaginians allowed them to go. Euthymenes, the explorer of the western African coasts, may well be earlier than Herodotus, and even than Hecataeus, as F. Jacoby suggested (P.-W., s.v.). The *Ora Maritima* by Avienus may be based on a Massaliote *periplous* of the sixth or fifth century B.C. (though this is a modern conjecture on shaky foundations). Pytheas, who probably lived in the fourth century, does not seem to have travelled inside Gaul. His enemies among the ancient geographers attacked him for what he reported about the mysterious North – Great Britain, Jutland, and whatever Thule was. But nobody attacked him for his information about France; which shows that he gave none. Until the second century B.C. the Greeks knew deplorably little about the Celtic world – and France in particular. Whatever information they had came from such second-hand reports as they were bound to pick up either in Marseilles or in Italy or in the Balkans, without having to visit the country for themselves. The first authorities we meet on the Celts, Ephorus and Timaeus, are typical armchair historians. They were pioneers, simply because the Massaliotes never made any effort to know their neighbours. Ephorus, who wrote his first books about 350 B.C., included the Celts in his description of the world. He put the Celts at one of the four corners of the world. They were philhellenes, fined young people who were too fat, and did not abandon their houses when they were invaded by water (Strabo 4.4.6, 7.2.1). Timaeus, who about 280 B.C. followed Ephorus in prefacing his history with a geographical introduction, was perhaps better informed. He could talk about the mouth of the river Rhône and about the influence of the Atlantic rivers on the tides of the ocean. He was interested in Massalia and must have reflected Massaliote opinions about the rest of Gaul. Polybius, who did not like Timaeus, admitted that he had taken trouble to get information about the West. No other writer of the late fourth or early third century could compete with either Ephorus or Timaeus about the Celts. Aristotle, no doubt, must have included them in his lost work on the customs of the barbarians. In his *Politics* he knew just enough to make sense of their institutions within the context of his classification. Though a military race, the Celts, unlike the Spartans, were not controlled by women, because they inclined to homosexuality; but, like the Spartans, they brought up their children austerely. Outside politics Aristotle has the usual mixture of odd bits of information – for instance that in certain parts of the Celtic land it is too cold for donkeys to procreate (*De gener. anim.* 2.8.748a). He does not seem to have done much research on Celts. But even Ephorus and Timaeus were later found to be superficial informants on them. Indeed, not even Eratosthenes presented what could be considered a decent amount of information according to the standards of later times. He is in fact specifically accused of ignorance about the Celts by Strabo (2.2.41). If one takes this attack by Strabo into account, it seems strange that specialists on the ancient sources about Gaul, such as P. Duval, can still believe that Eratosthenes wrote at least thirty-three books of *Galatica* on the Celts. One has simply to glance at the few fragments of these *Galatica* (745 Jacoby) – all quoted by Stephanus of Byzantium – to be persuaded that the author of the *Galatica* is a younger namesake of the great Eratosthenes – perhaps a descendant who noticed the lacunae in the geography of his predecessor. The *Galatica* by Eratosthenes were probably written *after* 156 B.C., because they allude to a war between Attalus II and Prusias. It is also certain that the number thirty-three in one of the quotations is a textual corruption: the *Galatica* may have had fewer books. Even so, they belong to the new era of Celtic studies which, as we shall soon see, was inaugurated and encouraged by the Romans.

Before the Romans came on the scene, the Greeks knew little about the Celts. Their geography, their institutions, and their economy were studied only from afar and superficially. The Greeks of Massalia, which would have been the obvious centre for the exploration of the Celtic world, never went beyond the coasts. Even the Druids emerged slowly and rather unexcitingly in the late third century B.C. in Sotion, the historian of Greek philosophy (Diog. Laertius, Introduction), and in a treatise on magic attributed by somebody to Aristotle, but more probably composed by the Peripatetic Antisthenes of Rhodes who lived about 200 B.C. (*Suda*). With all the interest in wise men of the barbarian world – Brahmans, Magi, Jewish and Egyptian priests – very little was made of the Druids. Sotion and Ps.-Aristotle quoted them to confirm the remote origin of philosophy outside the Greek world; but the main argument was represented by Magi and Brahmans who had a better and older reputation among Greek thinkers and historians (Diog. Laertius, Introd. 1).

Poor knowledge of the Celts does not mean that the Greeks were indifferent to them. They could hardly have afforded to be so. Since the beginning of the fourth century B.C. the Celts had been a factor to be reckoned with everywhere in the Mediterranean world. The first event of Roman history contemporary Greeks witnessed with interest, and perhaps with apprehension, was the sack of Rome by the Gauls. This was registered with due emphasis by Theopompus, Aristotle and Heraclides Ponticus. About 338 Scylax, or rather pseudo-Scylax (§ 18), noticed the presence of Celts on the Adriatic north of Ravenna in a region which was of direct commercial interest to the Greeks. Celtic mercenaries were enrolled by Dionysius the Elder in southern Italy. The Celts were pressing on the Macedonian frontiers at the time of Philip II and of Alexander the Great. Fifty years later they captured Delphi, if only for a brief period. Immediately afterwards they established themselves in Asia Minor – a constant source of trouble for all the powers concerned: Galatic mercenaries even conspired against Ptolemy II. Each of these interventions of the Celts proved their importance by producing major developments in the political systems which they attacked. Rome emerged as the greatest power in Italy when the Latins, for fear of the Celts, had to give up their independence about 350 B.C. The new kingdom of Macedonia under the firm hand of Antigonus Gonatas was the direct outcome of the Celtic invasion of Macedonia and Greece. The victory over the Galatians consolidated the state of Pergamum and probably provided Attalus I with the right occasion for declaring himself king. Finally it was Gnaeus Manlius Vulso's victory over the Galatians in 189 B.C.

which justified the intervention of the Romans in Asia Minor
and furnished them with the clients they needed in order to
control the ambitions of Pergamum. Hopeless in their attacks
against states defended by phalanx or legion, the Celts had
the numbers, the courage and the swiftness of the perfect
marauder.

The Greeks were too busy celebrating their victories
against the Celts in verse or marble to give serious thought to
the causes of such commotions. Patriotism and religion combined in what must surely be one of the most emotional
reactions of the Greeks to the impact of an alien society.
Though the sack of Delphi by the Celts is a legend, Apollo's
city had been in actual danger of being sacked. Religious
emotions led to the foundation of the *Soteria*, one of the most
important festivals of the Hellenistic world. An inscription
of Cos (*Syll.*³ 398) expresses the spontaneous enthusiasm of
the inhabitants of this island on learning the news of the
Gallic retreat from Delphi in 278; that was a day of victory
and salvation for the whole Greek world. Aratus wrote his
hymn to Pan after Antigonus Gonatas' victory over the Gauls
in the following year. Callimachus must have followed this
up with his epic poem *Galatea*, which (as Rudolf Pfeiffer
suggested) presented the Nereid Galatea as the mother of
Galatos, the ancestor of the Galatians (fr. 378-9 Pfeiffer).
Later Callimachus spoke of the 'foolish tribe of the Galatians' in his fourth hymn to Delos (l. 184) after Ptolemy
Philadelphus had punished his rebel Celtic mercenaries. The
Galatians even became an ingredient of comedy, to judge
from a fragment of the *Galatai* by Sopatros of Paphos, who
lived in Egypt about 280-270 B.C. (fr. 6 Kaibel). Every
Hellenistic hymn to Apollo came naturally to include an
allusion to the god's triumph over the Celts. Limenios' paean
inscribed at Delphi with its musical notation about 120 B.C.
still repeats the commonplace (Powell, *Collectanea Alexan-
drina*, 149). Other poets celebrated the victories of the
Seleucids and of the Attalids against the same barbarians.
According to the *Suda*, Simonides of Magnesia sang of a

victory by Antiochus III over the Gauls, about which we know nothing – unless it is to be identified with the episode to which II Maccabees refers as a success by eight thousand Babylonian Jews and four thousand Macedonians against Galatian raiders (8.20). A fragment of a poem in a Berlin papyrus edited by Wilamowitz alludes to an episode involving a Hellenistic king against the Gauls: the rest is left to our imagination (D. L. Page, *Greek Literary Papyri* I, 463).

Figurative arts, even more than poetry, expressed the mixed feelings of elation over past victories and fear of future incursions which the Celts inspired. Four episodes seem to have attracted the attention of the artists – or of their patrons. One was of course the attack on Delphi. Propertius saw 'deiectos Parnassi vertice Gallos' (Gauls hurled down from Parnassus) even on a door of the temple of Apollo on the Palatine (2.31.13). Another was the suicide of Brennus after his retreat from Delphi, which may be represented in a famous bronze of the museum of Naples. The third episode was the victory of Attalus I in 241 which was commemorated by initiative of the king himself, both in Pergamum and in Athens. Finally, Mario Segre in one of the most brilliant of his early studies argued that many of the Italian scenes with Gauls – such as the frieze of Città Alba in Picenum, which was discovered at the end of the last century – may represent a Celtic attack on the temple of Apollo and Artemis at Didyma near Miletus, which was sacked in 277/6 B.C. (*Studi Etruschi* 8 (1934), 137–42). Pergamene propaganda made the victory of Attalus pre-eminent. The kings of Pergamum, as the monument on the Athenian Acropolis shows, wished to appear as the protagonists of a new Gigantomachia – the defenders of the divine order of Hellenic civilization against the northern barbarians. Yet the artists engaged in these works were in no mood to present the barbarians as the incarnation of evil forces. They underlined the pain inflicted on the conquered Gauls and their courage in facing death – alone or with their families. The success with which these statues met shows that the public shared the feeling of the artists. Though we have no contemporary commentary on the Pergamene works we can hardly go wrong if we choose to see in them a monument to human pain made somehow more tolerable to contemplate because embodied in barbarians.

There were other more crude or more generic representations of the victories over the Celts. But it still remains significant that some of the pathetic figures are to be found on funerary urns. The visitor to the Museo Guarnacci of Volterra is not likely to forget the series of urns with strange scenes of marauding Celts who run away from a Fury. The Etruscans of the second century B.C. must have discovered some allegory of death in such episodes. On the other hand the south Italian potters of Cales must have found customers for their cups which through their imagery reminded the drinkers of the impious Celts in action: were they too a 'memento mori' or were they an invitation to rejoice in a world where barbarians are sure to be defeated?

The strong emotions provoked by the Celts became symbolic of human existence and developed in inverse proportion to the critical evaluation of Celtic society. We must of course make full allowance for the disappearance of the most important historical sources of the third century B.C. Hieronymus of Cardia is likely to have given a precise account of the Celtic events of 280–275 B.C. Later Phylarchus continued the story. We have two fragments by him (frs. 2 and 9 Jacoby) which can pass for Celtic ethnography; one is a tall story about a Celtic *potlatch*. But serious students of the Celtic world such as Strabo never refer to these third-century historians. We can see why, if we turn the pages of the only surviving detailed account of the Celtic invasion of 278 B.C. in Pausanias, Book 10. It has long been recognized that Pausanias gave a Herodotean dress and added some comments of his own to what must ultimately be a third-century B.C. account of the Celtic attack (O. Regenbogen, P.–W., s.v. Pausanias, Suppl. VIII, 1076). Now one of the comments of Pausanias is that before a battle the Celts neither employed a Greek soothsayer nor made sacrifices according to national custom – if indeed, as Pausanias pointedly remarks (10.21.1), there is such a thing as Celtic divination. What Pausanias implies is that he found nothing in his source about the Celtic art of divination which had been extolled by Posidonius and other authorities. Pausanias obviously enjoyed a dig at these famous scholars. But we shall not be surprised if in their turn the specialists refused to take seriously what they considered the uninformed accounts of writers like Pausanias' source. Indeed, Pausanias shows us what an account of a war with the Celts looked like in the pre-scientific days of Celtic studies, in the third century B.C. Direct contacts with the Celts seem to have been confined to prisoners or to mercenaries, bad subjects for ethnographic research.

III

The Romans had gone through similar emotions. For two centuries they had faced Celtic attacks. When they had decisively defeated the Gauls in the battle of Telamon in 225 B.C. they had commemorated the victory by a temple on the site, in which the Celts appeared as the modern counterpart of the Seven against Thebes. The Romans entered the *tumultus gallicus* in their laws as a recognized emergency. The levy in mass against the Gauls is still mentioned in the charter granted to the 'colonia Genetiva Julia' in Spain in 44 B.C., when it was presumably a simple piece of antiquarianism, if it did not allude to Caesar's recent wars. But since the beginning of the third century B.C. the Romans had also started a policy of occupation of Gallic territory. This occupation (at least with the Senones of the Adriatic coast and the Boii north of the Apennines) was at first equivalent to an extermination of Celtic tribes. Slowly, however, the Romans had to learn to govern Celts, and this became an even more pressing responsibility when Spain was organized in two provinces in 197 B.C. For three centuries the Romans were steadily engaged – among their multifarious commitments –

in annexing territories which were partially or totally Celtic until they came to control the greater part of the Celtic-speaking world. They became interested in the peculiarities of the Celtic society they tried to control and subdue.

Cato the Censor fought as a very young man at the battle of the Metaurus where Hasdrubal had been heavily supported by Gaulish troops. He started his political career at the time when the Cenomani of Brixia answered the call to rebellion from the last Punic commander in Italy, Hamilcar. He was in Spain as a consul in 195 to lay the foundations of the Roman administration. He reported about Cantabrian customs (fr. 94 Peter). Cato had an instinctive interest and perhaps respect for the conquered populations of Italy and the provinces. He observed the Celts with care and seems to have been the first to find them witty: 'pleraque Gallia duas res industriosissime persequitur, rem militarem et argute loqui' (fr. 34 Peter). The emendation of 'argute loqui' into 'agriculturam' proposed by a distinguished Celtic scholar must be the least argute emendation of any text (G. Dottin, *Mélanges L. Havet* (1909), 119). The Celts loomed large in Cato's *Origines*. He tried to achieve clarity on places and names. He found a branch of the dangerous Cenomani among the Volcae not far from Marseilles. He was probably the first to include the Gauls in a history of Italy, though Fabius Pictor who fought against them in 225 B.C. was bound to have said something about their characteristics. The example of Cato must have been decisive. While Cato was still alive the Roman governing class made a determined effort to get to know the Celts better. Much could be learnt from day by day contacts. But the science of geography was Greek. If the Romans wanted systematic information about the Celtic lands and institutions they had to recruit Greek scholars. Under Augustus or Tiberius Strabo still stated, as an evident fact, that in the study of little-known countries 'the Roman writers are imitators of the Greeks and they do not carry their imitation very far, for what they relate they merely translate from the Greeks' (3.4.19). The Greeks worked hard to describe the Celtic world of Spain and Gaul in the service of Roman expansion. What they had not done when the Celts were plundering Greece and Asia Minor, they did later for the benefit of the Romans. Greek technicians probably helped in the routine work of mapping the conquered countries. One likes to think that Demetrius 'the topographer', who put Ptolemy Philometor up when he went to Rome as a suppliant, made his precarious living by this kind of work (Diodor. 31.18). But what the Romans really needed from the Greeks was the description and interpretation of a foreign land as a whole; they lacked orientation in ethnography.

Polybius was available. Even Cato could not conceal a grudging sympathy for him. Polybius travelled in Celtic lands under Roman auspices and with Roman help and protection. The details are notoriously uncertain. He probably went twice to Spain with Scipio Aemilianus, in 151 and in 134; on his first journey he must have visited southern France, including Marseilles (Polyb. 3.59.7). Between these two journeys, in 147–6, he was given ships by Scipio to explore the coasts of Africa (Plin. *N.H.* 5.9–10). It is not impossible that on this sea voyage he was accompanied by Panaetius, who, according to a very fragmentary and dubious passage of the *Index Stoicorum*, apparently travelled by sea with Scipio at about this time (col. 56, ed. Traversa p. 78). Polybius was the first to give a first-hand account of the interior of Spain. He described Gaul – or at least southern Gaul – in a way which represented a novelty for the Greek public (3.59.7). We can see how he used his knowledge for the chapters on Hannibal in Gaul of Book 3 of his histories; but Book 24 in which he summarized his findings is lost. When he claimed in Book 12 that, contrary to Timaeus, he had taken the trouble to visit the lands of the Ligurians and of the Gauls, he was being true to the facts. But at least in Book 3 and in Book 12 he forgot to say that his explorations were made possible by the Romans and would benefit the Romans. Cato had realistically encouraged the Romans to do

what no Greek had done before – to study the Celts in their
own land. Now we see how the Roman leading class accepted his advice and hired the Greeks to do the work for them.

It is impossible to say whether the younger Eratosthenes
(*F.Gr.H.* no. 745 Jacoby) who wrote his books on Gaul
about this time, 150 B.C., had been encouraged by the
Romans. A younger Callisthenes quoted as an authority on
Gaul by Ps.-Plutarch, *De fluviis* 6.1 (= Jacoby, no. 291, 5)
is said to have been born in southern Italy, that is, in territory
under Roman control. But like many other authors quoted
by Ps.-Plutarch, he may never have existed. We can be more
definite about Artemidorus of Ephesus and Posidonius of
Rhodes whom Strabo treated as his most authoritative sources
for Spain and Gaul. Both were ambassadors to Rome for their
own cities – that is, they were very acceptable to the governing class of Rome. In his celebrated visit to Posidonius' house
in Rhodes, Pompey made it clear that the Roman fasces had
to bow down before philosophy; they certainly had nothing
to fear from it. It is evident that Artemidorus and Posidonius
travelled in Spain and Gaul with the support of the Roman
authorities. In any case, the situation was such that the
Romans were bound to derive advantage from their observations. Artemidorus wrote before Posidonius, who occasionally disagreed with him: he must have travelled about 100
B.C. He seems to have done particularly useful work on the
geography of Spain where he had the advantage of a century
of Roman administration. But he had ethnographic remarks
to make about both Spain (Strabo 3.4.17) and Gaul (4.4.6),
and he seems to have prepared the way for the far more com-
prehensive enquiry of Posidonius.

Whatever may be our private feelings about the modern
scholarship on Posidonius, one of its most durable results is
the reconstruction of Posidonius' chapters on the Celts. A few
impressive verbatim quotations by Athenaeus and some references in Strabo were the starting point. The discovery that
Diodorus V contained a paraphrase of the same basic text
gave an altogether different dimension to Posidonius' work.

After that, it was easier to see that Strabo himself largely depended on Posidonius and that Caesar, too, must have used Posidonius in the ethnographic excursuses of the *Bellum Gallicum*.

For many years the dependence of Strabo on Posidonius was obscured by the theory of Alfred Klotz (*Caesarstudien*, 1910) that Strabo used Posidonius only indirectly through his older contemporary Timagenes. It was an unlikely theory even at first sight. Strabo quotes Timagenes only once (4.1.13) to say that Posidonius was right and Timagenes was wrong on the origins of the *aurum tolosanum*, the gold from Tolosa which ruined the career of Caepio. It is difficult to infer from this passage that Strabo trusted Timagenes about the Celts and never made use of the original text of Posidonius – who had been directly or indirectly his own teacher. Strabo had an independent mind. If he did not copy Timagenes, he should not be suspected of having copied Posidonius. He was acquainted with many sources of the Caesarian and Augustan age; he even quotes Caesar's *Commentarii* (4.1.1). It is furthermore clear that when he expressed a favourable judgement on the Romanization of Spain and Gaul he was not copying what his most recent editor, F. Lasserre, has imagined to be a panegyric of Augustus. Strabo himself was the apologist. That much said, it remains true that Strabo never went north of Populonia in Etruria, knew little Latin and was bound to depend on written Greek sources for his account of the Celtic lands. We are fortunate in his choice of Posidonius as his main source.

Posidonius wrote a monograph about the Oceans. But what he wrote on the Celts was mainly to be found in the history of the period *circa* 146–80, and in his books on Pompey's wars. He wrote *because* of the Roman progress in Spain and in Gaul, and therefore in full awareness of the new reality. If he appears to have produced a static image of Celtic society, as if the Roman impact was not yet to be observed, he must have known what he was doing. Posidonius was capable of recognizing a change when he saw one. His approach to the Celts was deliberate; he intended to preserve the physiognomy of a world in danger of disappearing. At least in one case he almost says so – in the history of Lovernius, to which I shall return.

Ancient ethnography gives little space to language. Comparative philology had not been invented. Ethnic groups were defined in terms of common descent and of common institutions. Posidonius was not a discoverer of a new ethnographical method. But he was very systematic in his descriptions and had a rare gift for the significant detail. Furthermore, he needed amusement and knew how to get it. He loved the hierarchical structure of Celtic society because it was hierarchical, but also because it was extravagant. The Rhodian aristocratic merchants among whom he lived had hierarchy, but not extravagance. Posidonius enjoyed describing those strictly hierarchical banquets of the Celts in which people challenged each other to mortal duels on fine points of honour, such as the best piece of meat. He contemplated with relish large retinues of clients singing the praises of their patrons. Permanent clientship was a good thing. It gave the Celts delightful chieftains, such as Lovernius who entertained hugely: 'And when at length he fixed a day for the ending of the feast, a Celtic poet who arrived too late met Lovernius and composed a song magnifying his greatness and lamenting his own late arrival. Lovernius was very pleased and asked for a bag of gold and threw it to the poet who ran beside his chariot. The poet picked it up and sang another song...' (Athenaeus 4.37, p. 152). Alas, there was no chance of another Lovernius. As Posidonius remarks in passing, he was 'the father of Bituis who was dethroned by the Romans'. Posidonius confessed that at first he had been disturbed by the spectacle of human heads nailed up at the entrance of the aristocratic Celtic houses, but afterwards 'becoming used to it he could bear it with equanimity' (Strabo 4.4.5).

It was Posidonius who defined the place of the Druids,

the *vates*, and the bards in Celtic society. All the later tradition virtually depends on him. Here again he was alerted by a long tradition of Greek search for barbarian philosophers and seers. But his sympathy for the Druids, the *vates* and the bards implies an authentic recognition of their function in the Celtic world. The Druids were for Posidonius more important than the other two groups because they provided leadership, moral and religious ideas, and justice. They preserved something of the golden age when, as Seneca says, 'penes sapientes fuisse regnum Posidonius indicat' (*Ep.* 90). When we read in Strabo, certainly from Posidonius, that the Druids 'have pronounced that men's souls and the universe are indestructible, although at times fire or water may temporarily prevail' (4.4.4), it is easy to suspect that Posidonius attributed ordinary Stoic doctrines to his Druids. Yet the situation is not so simple. Posidonius had to interpret the strong belief in the other world which we know from independent evidence to have existed among the Celts of his time. Furthermore, even before Posidonius, the Druids may well have heard about Greek doctrines of immortality either from oral tradition in Massalia or by honest purchase of Greek books. They cared for learning. Later, if we are to believe Cicero, *De divinatione* 1.90, his friend and guest, the Druid Divitiacus, gave answers in perfect Posidonian style: 'et naturae rationem quam φυσιολογίαν Graeci appellant, notam esse sibi profitebatur'. Perhaps Divitiacus had read his Posidonius – or somebody had read Posidonius to him. For it must be remembered that Divitiacus does not seem to have been in perfect command either of Greek or of Latin. Caesar used an interpreter in his formal meeting with him about his brother Dumnorix (*B.G.* 1.19).

Druidism was, however, only a small portion of Posidonius' picture of Celtic society, and we must ask ourselves what impression such a picture would make on his contemporaries. As for his Greek readers, the only certain fact is that he was famous enough to be copied – or summarized

– by his younger contemporary Diodorus. But after the sack
of Athens by Sulla and the destruction of the Seleucid state
by Pompey the taste for the quiet contemplation of world
history which Posidonius encouraged must have been confined to provincial corners like Rhodes itself, or Agyrium,
the Sicilian birthplace of Diodorus.

The reaction in Latium is more distinctly recognizable. It
includes the significant silence of Cicero who knew his
Posidonius. Cicero denigrated the Gauls in the *Pro Fonteio*
about 69 B.C. because his client Fonteius had been accused
by them. He did not need to turn to Posidonius for his cheap
ethnography – assuming, what is by no means certain, that
about 69 B.C. Posidonius' history had already been published. Later, as far as we know, Cicero never seriously returned to the subject of the Celtic society – not even in his
speech for Caesar *De provinciis consularibus*. Books, and
there are so many of them, on Cicero's political thought
might at least note the desperate vagueness of his ideas on
the provincials, which in the case of the Gauls amounted
to contempt. Varro studied the Celts and appeared to St
Jerome to be a great authority on them (*P.L.* 26.353).
Posidonius was of course behind him. Perhaps encouraged
by Varro, Caesar went to conquer Gaul with Posidonius in
his satchel. The ethnographical excursuses of the *Bellum
Gallicum*, which few nowadays would consider inter-
polated, are similar in content and style to the Posidonian
sections of Diodorus and Strabo. Notice that Caesar never
mentions the Druids except in the long ethnographic digres-
sion of Book 6.11–28. He did not encounter the Druids in
his campaigns, but in his literary sources – whatever the
explanation of their absence from the battlefield may be.

As Caesar wrote his ethnography towards the end of the
war, he was in a position to mix his own observations with
what he found in his sources. Any attempt to separate the
old and the new is hopeless. But in its broad outlines his
image of the Celtic society coincides with that of Posidonius.
Like Posidonius he stresses the internal factions and the

strife of the Celts, and the volatile character of their deci-
sions. Michel Rambaud took all the passages in which
Caesar mentioned the 'mobilitas et levitas animi' (2.1.3),
the 'Gallorum subita et repentina consilia' (3.8.3), the
'Gallorum infirmitas' (4.13.3) etc. as typical examples of
'déformation historique' (*La déformation historique dans
les Commentaires de César* (Paris, 1953), 326). If it was a
deformation, it was anticipated by Posidonius. Caesar found
in him not only valuable factual information about places
and institutions, but an encouraging analysis of the weak-
ness of Celtic society.

It is certainly a paradox that Posidonius, the friend and
protégé of Pompey, should help Caesar through his historical work to conquer Gaul and therefore to destroy his
rival.

As we have tried to explain, the exploitation of Greek
ethnography by Roman leaders had started much earlier.
The Celts had been sadly overlooked by the Greeks. When
they invaded Greek territories emotions prevailed over
analysis. The systematic study of Celtic lands was made by
Greeks under the Roman hegemony and with Roman en-
couragement. Now we can see the results. The importance
of the names involved – Polybius, Artemidorus, Posidonius
– corresponds to the magnitude of the prize. It was by
conquering the Celts, in Italy, Gaul, Spain, Britain and
Danubian countries, that the Roman Empire consolidated
itself as a world power. It was also in the Celtic countries
that Romanization celebrated its most truculent triumph.
Celtic civilization was wiped out or driven underground.

The Druids re-emerged in the nostalgia of the Gallic
aristocrats of the fourth century and in the irresponsible
imagination of the *Scriptores Historiae Augustae*. Remark-
ably enough, female Druids, not documented before, prevailed in these late phantasies. There may be more than
mere nostalgia in all this. Celtae was the name of one of the
best units in Julian's army (Ammianus 20.4.2), and Julian
himself says that it was inconceivable to all men that a

Celtic or Galatian soldier should turn his back to the enemy (*Orat.* 1, *Paneg. Const.* 36в). Claudian repeats the claim (*Bell. Gild.* 1.431): 'Sitque palam Gallos causa, non robore vinci.' Celtic self-awareness may be traced in the popular rebellions of the fifth century, especially in Armorica (Zosim. 6.5.3). A desire to remind Rome of its arrogance remained latent in the Celtic underground. It received its best expression in that story of the *Mabinogion* about 'The Dream of Macsen Wledig', the dream of the Emperor Maximus. As you will remember, the Emperor Maximus, having married the British princess Elen, remained in this island for seven years and therefore lost his right to return to Rome. A new emperor was elected. Maximus tried to reconquer Rome but failed and had to call in the help of his British brothers-in-law. The Britons observed that 'every-day at midday the two (rival) emperors would take their meat, and on both sides they would cease fighting till all had finished eating. But the men of the Island of Britain took their meat in the morning and drank till they were in-spirited. And while the two emperors were at meat the Britons approached the rampart and planted their ladders against it' (transl. Gwyn and Thomas Jones, Everyman, p. 86). The rest is obvious. Here for the first time a Celtic writer proclaimed the superiority of British early breakfast over Latin siesta.

4

The Hellenistic discovery of Judaism

I

The Greeks were perhaps the first to study the peculiarities of foreigners. They began by collecting information as traders or colonists but by the end of the sixth century B.C. they were already writing books on ethnography and geography to satisfy their taste for enquiry – for *historia*, as they called it. As Herodotus shows, their enquiries extended to territories no Greek had ever visited (4.25). On the other hand we have noticed that the Greeks were much less curious than we would expect them to be about certain countries within their reach and indeed well inside their sphere of economic and cultural influence. Their interest in Celtic lands and civilization became apparent only in the fourth century B.C., though they had founded the important colony of Marseilles as early as the end of the seventh century. Even more paradoxically, that distinguished son of Marseilles, Pytheas, who discovered the north of Europe, seems never to have travelled inside France. The historians Ephorus and Timaeus, who in the fourth and third centuries B.C. were the first to collect extensive information about Gaul and Spain, do not seem ever to have visited these countries.

Ancient travellers did not find it easy to go into the interior of countries. We must consequently not expect Greek callers at Palestinian ports to go up to Jerusalem for the pleasure of observing Jewish festivals. But trade relations between Greeks of some sort and Palestinians started in the

74

Mycenaean period; Greek mercenaries represented another point of contact.

It is probable that David employed Cretan mercenaries (II Sam. 20.23; I Kings 1.38); they presumably spoke Greek. About 840 Joash was put on the throne either by Carian or by Cretan mercenaries, according to which interpretation one prefers of II Kings 11.4. Greek ships with Greek traders certainly reappeared along the coasts of Palestine in the ninth and eighth centuries B.C. At Samaria Greek pottery antedates the destruction of the city by Sargon II in 722. At Tall Sukas between Tripolis and Laodikeia (Latakia), the Danish excavator P. J. Riis found a Greek settlement with a temple which seems to have been built in the seventh century and rebuilt about 570 B.C. The Greeks remained at Tall Sukas at least until 500 B.C. to trade with Palestinians of any religious and national variety. There were Greek mercenaries in the Egyptian army of Necho son of Psammetichus who killed Josiah – allegedly at Megiddo – in 608 B.C. There were thirty thousand Greeks, according to Herodotus, in the army of Necho's grandson Apries who tried to relieve Babylonian pressure on Palestine in 588 (Jerem. 37.5) and probably precipitated the final onslaught of Nebuchadnezzar on Jerusalem in 586 B.C. It has even been suggested that a king of Judah had Greek mercenaries. The excavations by J. Naveh at Mesad Hashavyahu, not far from Yavneh in central Judaea, yielded a great deal of Greek pottery from the last decades of the seventh century. The place looks like a fortress and may have been occupied by Greek mercenaries rather than by Greek traders. When Jeremiah fled to Egypt he went to Tahpanhes (43.7; 44.1) which was known to the Greek world under the name of Daphne and was probably already garrisoned by Greek mercenaries, as it certainly was a little later under King Amasis (570–526). It is tempting to imagine Jeremiah being received by Greek soldiers on Egyptian soil.

Contacts survived the exile. Finds of Greek pottery at Bet-Zur on the road from Jerusalem to Hebron are signs

of brisk trade in the first part of the fifth century. Attic
sherds of En-gedi belong mainly to the late fifth and early
fourth centuries. We know from the orator Isaeus that an
Athenian mercenary had accumulated a fortune of two
talents at Akko about 370 B.C. (4.7). The earliest coins of
Judaea imitate Greek coins in the interest of trade with the
Greeks. We do not know what authority was responsible for
them. Money of Yavan – of Greece – it will be remembered,
is mentioned in one of the papyri, dated 402 B.C., of
the Jewish colony of Elephantine in Egypt (*Brooklyn Pap.*
12).

The Jews had other opportunities for contacting Greeks in
Mesopotamia as well as in Egypt. It is symbolic that a Babylonian text records a payment of oil to Jehoiakin, the son of
the king of Judah, and to seven Greek carpenters who
worked for the Babylonian court (*Ancient Near Eastern
Texts*, 2 ed., p. 308). In Egypt native and Persian kings
attracted not only Greek and Carian but also Jewish mercenaries. The origins of the military colony of Elephantine
are unknown, but the author of the letter which goes under
the name of Aristeas must have found somewhere the piece
of information that Jewish soldiers helped Psammetichus in
his campaign against the king of the Ethiopians (13). The
Psammetichus in question is Psammetichus II who had the
support of Greeks, Carians and perhaps Phoenicians in his
expedition of 589 against Nubia. The graffiti left by these
soldiers at Abu Simbel in Lower Nubia are famous. If the
information of Aristeas is correct, Jewish and Greek soldiers
must have rubbed shoulders in the same campaign. The
absence of Hebrew graffiti at Abu Simbel is perhaps not
sufficient to throw doubt upon Aristeas. A recent papyro-
logical discovery shows that in the fourth century B.C. a
story like the judgement of Solomon was known in Greece
(*Pap. Oxy.* 2944), but there is no sign that it came from the
Bible.

Such being the direct evidence for contacts between
Greeks and Jews before the time of Alexander, we ask the

obvious question: what did Greeks and Jews make of these various opportunities for meeting and knowing each other? As for the Greeks, the answer is simple. They did not register the existence of the Jews. The little nation which was later to present the most radical challenge to the wisdom of the Greeks is mentioned nowhere in the extant pre-Hellenistic texts. The absence of references to Jews in Greek literature disturbed Hellenized Jews, as we can read in the Letter of Aristeas (31; 312). Flavius Josephus made a diligent search for references to Jews in Greek literature when he compiled his *contra Apionem*; and no doubt he had many predecessors in this hunt. The results were negligible. The most ancient author Josephus could find was the poet Choerilus, a contemporary of Herodotus. Choerilus mentioned Solymian mountains inhabited by warriors speaking the Phoenician language. Unfortunately, the tonsure Choerilus attributed to these people was explicitly forbidden to the Jews by Mosaic Law (Lev. 19.27), which was clearly in operation at the time of Jeremiah (Jer. 9.26). It is practically certain that Choerilus had in mind the eastern Ethiopians, and that he combined several passages from Homer (*Odys.* 5.283) and from Herodotus (7.79; 7.89 and possibly 3.8) to form his fanciful picture. Nor does Herodotus necessarily refer to the Jews when he mentions Syrians and Phoenicians of Palestine, who acknowledge that they learnt circumcision from the Egyptians (2.104).

Modern scholars who have tried to imitate Josephus in his search for references to Jews in pre-Alexandrian Greek literature have had no better luck. A fragment of the poet Alcaeus (50 Diehl = 27 Lobel–Page) has been taken to imply that his brother Antimenides fought against a gigantic Jew during one of the two sieges of Jerusalem by Nebuchadnezzar. But S. Luria – who proposed, or rather re-proposed this conjecture (*Acta Antiqua* 8 (1960), 265–6) – had to postulate that Alcaeus called Jerusalem Hierosylyma, not Hierosolyma, and his only evidence for this was an etymological joke with antisemitic undertones quoted by Josephus (*c. Apionem* 1.311), according to which the word Hiero-solyma came from *hierosylos*, 'temple robber'. No doubt Antimenides fought in Palestine for the Babylonians, but his brother Alcaeus was not interested in specifying against whom he fought. Another text with allusions to Jewish ethical norms attributed to Phocylides was recognized long ago to be a Jewish forgery of the Hellenistic age. Franz Dornseiff – a German scholar who proved his courage and independence in difficult times – tried hard to persuade us that it was in fact authentic Greek poetry of the sixth century B.C. He also tried to show that a long description of the Jews attributed by Photius to Hecataeus of Miletus was really composed by this late sixth-century writer, and not (as is generally admitted) by the younger Hecataeus of Abdera who lived after Alexander. In both cases Dornseiff failed to convince. These texts attributed to Phocylides and to Hecataeus of Miletus are at least two centuries later – with the difference that 'Phocylides' covers a forgery, whereas 'Hecataeus of Miletus' is a wrong attribution, little more than a slip of the pen. Nothing so far has disproved the contention that the classical Greeks did not even know the name of the Jews.

In short, as far as we know, the Greeks lived happily in their classical age without recognizing the existence of the Jews. As for the Jews of the biblical period, they of course knew of Yavan, which designated all the Greeks rather than specifically the Ionians. Where Yavan is more precisely defined, as in the genealogy of Noah, Yavan is father of Elisah, Tarsis, Kittim and Dodanim; that is, probably, of Alashiya and Kition in Cyprus, of Rhodes and of Tarsus – rather than Tartessus. There is no indication that Athens, Sparta, Thebes or even Miletus and Ephesus were consciously connected with the name Yavan. This table of the Nations in Genesis 10 can hardly be more ancient than the seventh century B.C. Not much later Ezechiel or one of his disciples included Yavan in the lamentation for Tyre (27.13–19). Here Yavan is one of the merchants who trade with Tyre, and slaves are among the merchandise. Ezechiel's motif of the Greeks as merchants is taken up by Joel who accuses Tyre and Sidon and 'all the coasts of Palestine' – that is the Philistines – of trading with Yavan and of selling them 'the children of Judah and the children of Jerusalem' (3.6). It is a well-known problem whether Joel – or at least this section of Joel – belongs to the post-exilic period. Yavan is mentioned in the last chapter of Isaiah, 66.19, among the peoples to whom God will reveal his glory. This is probably a late sixth-century text. Finally, Yavan appears in the Messianic promise of Zechariah 9.13: 'I have raised up thy sons of Zion, against thy sons of Greece.' But this text clearly belongs to the period after Alexander, though I would not commit myself to a Maccabean date. The few biblical texts with the mention of Yavan which can be dated with probability before 336 b.c. know the Greeks only as traders – or more generically as one of the nations of the world. The Greeks are known, but they appear rather remote and insignificant. In the pre-Hellenistic sections of the Bible there is no notion that can be ascribed to Greek influence: indeed there is no certain Greek word. The first certain Greek words in the Bible are in the Book of Daniel (3.5), which in its present form belongs to the third and second centuries b.c. It is furthermore probable that in Kohelet (Ecclesiastes) the Persian word *pardes* (2.5) is used in a meaning, orchard, given to it by the Greeks under the form παράδεισος. But Kohelet, too, is probably Hellenistic.

The picture does not really change if we turn from the Bible to those seals and bronzes from the Persian period with which the Archaeological Museums of Jerusalem have made us familiar. There we meet Athena, Heracles, satyrs and other Greek deities. We do not know who were the owners, nor what the objects meant to the owners. Those of us who display Buddha in the drawing-room are not necessarily Buddhists. There is indeed no indication that any Jew ever worshipped a Greek god before Alexander. This is interesting, because we know that even in the post-exilic period a considerable proportion of the Jews was for all practical purposes polytheistic. Pure monotheism was by then securely established in the Second Temple of Jerusalem, but remained shaky elsewhere. During and after the exile Ezechiel (33.23), the Third Isaiah (57.1–10; 65.11–12) and the Second Zechariah (10.2; 13.2) denounced the worship of idols, the slaying of children, and the practice of ritual prostitution. In the Babylonian Murashu documents of the fifth century B.C. unmistakably Jewish names alternate in the same family with Babylonian theophoric names. The colonists of Elephantine in Egypt combined observance of the Passover and perhaps of the Sabbath with a devotion to Eshembethel and Anathbethel which my late colleague and friend Umberto Cassuto was unable to explain away. Greek gods are conspicuous by their absence in these documents of the declining Jewish polytheism of the fifth century B.C.

One document still defies interpreters. I allude of course to the mysterious figure on a coin now in the British Museum. The coin belongs to the Persian period, bears the inscription 'Judaea' (YHD), and shows a figure on a winged throne or on a chariot: this figure apparently confronts a Dionysiac mask (B. Kanael, *The Biblical Archaeologist* 26 (1963), 40 and fig. 2). This is something unique; and it is not surprising that somebody should have thought of the mystical chariot of Ezechiel. I am sure that everyone in this room satisfies the Rabbinic condition for discussing the chariot of Ezechiel (*ma'ase merkava*) – namely to be wise and able to deduce knowledge through wisdom of his own – but I do not propose to indulge in this subject. All the other Judaean coins of the Persian period have non-Jewish symbols; there is no particular reason to believe that this coin bears a Jewish symbol. As I have already said, we do not know under what authority the coins were issued.

Before Alexander the Jews knew a little more about the Greeks than the Greeks knew about the Jews. After all, the Greeks traded in Palestine, but apparently no Jew traded in Greece. This difference did not amount to any assimilation

of Greek culture among the Jews. Yet the developments
which took place in Judaea in the fifth and fourth centuries
B.C. offer many points of comparison with contemporary
Greek developments. Both Greeks and Jews were living on
the borders of the Persian Empire. Nehemiah's work can best
be understood if compared with Greek events. In political
terms Nehemiah was a tyrant imposed by the Persians just
as much as Histiaeus and others had been imposed as tyrants
over Greek cities by the Persian government. Nehemiah
rebuilt Jerusalem, as Themistocles had to rebuild Athens.
His remission of debts had obvious analogies in Greek
practice of the sixth and fifth centuries. Nehemiah's law
against mixed marriages was paralleled in Athens by Pericles' legislation against foreign wives. Even Ezra's and
Nehemiah's autobiographies were new in Judaea, as Ion of
Chios' memoirs were new in Greece – practically at the same
time. E. Bickerman once compared the work of the Chronicler with that of Herodotus. It was perhaps a wrong comparison. The technique by which in the fourth century B.C.
the Chronicler rewrote and modernized the Books of Kings
reminds us of the technique by which in the late fourth
century Ephorus and Theopompus rewrote and modernized
Herodotus and Thucydides. Other parallels can be adduced
and have been adduced. The table of the Nations in Genesis
10 reminds us of the map of Anaximander; the Book of
Job, probably an exilic work, has often been compared with
Aeschylus' *Prometheus*.

One can speculate why, with so much in common, Greeks
and Jews do not seem to have spoken to each other. One
explanation is only too obvious. They had no language in
common. The Greeks were monolingual; the Jews were bilingual, but their second language, Aramaic, gave them
access to Persians and Babylonians, even to Egyptians, rather
than to Greeks. Yet language difficulties have never been
insurmountable barriers. Perhaps we have to reckon with an
element of chance. Herodotus did not happen to visit Jerusalem. A page of Herodotus would have been sufficient

to put a battalion of biblical scholars out of action. Ultimately, however, we must perhaps admit deeper obstacles.
Under the guidance of Nehemiah and his successors the
Jews were intent on isolating themselves from the surrounding nations. They trusted in God and his Law. For the
same purpose, the Greeks trusted their own intelligence and
initiative, were unceremoniously aggressive and contributed
everywhere to disturbing the peace of the Persian Empire on
which the reconstruction of Judaism depended. One hundred and twenty years after Nehemiah and Pericles Greeks
and Jews found themselves under the control of Alexander
the Great – a Greek-speaking Macedonian who considered
himself the heir of the Persian kings.

II

We have no idea of how the Jews reacted to the news that
Persepolis was burning. Alexander never went to Jerusalem.
But Jewish legends which found their way into the Alexander romance fondly narrated the encounter between the
High Priest and the new King of Kings. Jewish legend also
suggested that Alexander proclaimed the unity of God from
the tower of his new city, Alexandria (Ps.-Callisth. ii, 28,
p. 84 Müller). In Christian writers there is a story, probably
of Jewish origin, that Alexander brought the bones of the
prophet Jeremiah into Alexandria to keep snakes and croco-
diles out of it (*Suda*, s.v. Ἀργόλαι). These legends prove at
least that in Palestine the transition from the Persian to the
Macedonian rule had been smooth. The memory of Alexander remained one of those pieces of folklore the Jews could
share with their neighbours.

Alexander had certainly done one thing for the Jews
which proved to be irreversible. He put the majority of them
into a Greek-speaking, instead of an Aramaic-speaking,
world. After his death Palestine was a bone of contention
for more than twenty years. One of the rivals for the succession, Ptolemy, occupied Jerusalem in 320 – perhaps by

taking advantage of the Sabbath (Joseph. *Antiq.* 12.5 and *c. Apion.* 1.205; Appian. *Syr.* 50). From 301 to 198 the Ptolemies ruled Palestine. Greco-Macedonian governors, soldiers and traders came to live in Palestine by right of conquest. Philosophers and historians looked into Jerusalem, and, on the whole, they were pleased. Judaism became suddenly known – and respectable.

The conquerors of the Persian Empire found it advisable to get to know and, if possible, to win over the natives. Not everywhere had the previous rulers been popular. The Egyptians had a most successful record of rebellions against the Persians; the Babylonians had repeatedly revolted. Even in Palestine, where the Persians had been good rulers, there had been troubles, if our confused evidence is to be trusted at all (*c. Apion.* 1.194; Syncellus 1, 486A). The Greco-Macedonians tried to present themselves as more sympathetic masters than their predecessors. They were helped by trends of thought which had developed in Greece in the fourth century. Here the interrelation between ideology and action is particularly complex. Platonic and Pythagorean philosophy had prepared the Greeks to understand and appreciate rigorously hierarchic, indeed hieratic, communities. The philosopher-king was not far removed from the priest-king. Platonists were aware of Zoroaster. The historian Theopompus wrote on him. Alexander's teacher Aristotle did not share this liking for priests, but his scientific curiosity which was truly universal extended to the wisdom of the East. We shall meet several Aristotelians in our path.

Thus the new interest and sympathy were not specifically directed towards the Jews. But the other barbarians – Egyptians, Persians, Babylonians and even Indians – had been known to the Greeks for centuries. There was much previous information available, now to be reassessed and brought up to date. The Jews were the newcomers. Everything had still to be learnt about them. It is perhaps not by chance that the first Greek book to speak extensively about the Jews was written by an adviser of Ptolemy I in the years in which he was campaigning for the conquest of Palestine. Hecataeus of Abdera included a section on the Jews in a book about Egypt which he wrote in Egypt before 300 B.C., probably about 315 B.C. Hecataeus idealized the Egyptians and especially their priestly class. He spoke about the Jews in an Egyptian context, though the fragment preserved by Diodorus and quoted by Photius does not allow us to see the exact place of the Jewish excursus in the plan of his book. According to Hecataeus, the Jews were among the people – including the illustrious Danaus and Cadmus – who had been expelled by the Egyptians during a pestilence. Moses, a man distinguished by wisdom and courage, had guided the emigration, founded Jerusalem, built the Temple, divided the people into twelve tribes, established the priesthood and altogether enacted praiseworthy laws. He had ensured a large population by making the land inalienable and by prohibiting the exposure of children, a practice common among the Greeks. He had prescribed an education of almost Spartan rigour; the comparison with Sparta is obvious, but only implicit. If the type of life Moses had introduced was slightly unsocial and hostile to strangers, this was understandable after the painful experience of leaving Egypt. Hecataeus ended his excursus by noticing, in conformity with a well-known pattern of Greek ethnography, that the Jews had modified their customs under the influence of Persian and Macedonian rule. Hecataeus did not know of the patriarchs and apparently had never heard of Hebrew kings. One of the intriguing features of his account is that he seems to have heard or read at least one quotation in Greek from the Pentateuch. He says that at the end of the Laws of Moses one finds the following words: 'Moses, having heard the words of God, transmitted them to the Jews.' This seems to be an echo of Deuteronomy 29.1. A pre-Septuagint translation of some sections of the Torah is not altogether incredible and is, in any case, given as a fact by Aristobulus, an Alexandrian Jew writing in Greek during the second century B.C. (Eusebius, *Praep. Ev.* 13.12.1).

More or less in the same years about 300 B.C. the greatest
pupil of Aristotle, Theophrastus, became interested in
Jewish customs within the context of his comparative re-
searches on Piety. Jacob Bernays was the first to notice, in
1866, that a fragment of Theophrastus' book *On Piety* concerning the Jews was quoted by Porphyry in his treatise *On
Abstinence* (2.26). Theophrastus spoke of the Jews as philosophers who had by now discarded human sacrifice and performed their holocausts while fasting and talking inces-
santly about God. Besides, the Jews inspected the stars by
night, turned their eyes towards them and invoked them in
their prayers.

The notion that the Jews were philosophers recurs in a
book about India by Megasthenes who was an ambassador
to that country on behalf of Seleucus I in about 292 and
who reported what he had seen. His idea that the Jews were
to the Syrians what the Brahmans were to the Indians
gained favour (*F.Gr.H.* 715 F.3 Jacoby). Clearchus of Soli,
another pupil of Aristotle, who must have read his Megasthenes, went a step further and suggested that the Jews were
in fact the descendants of the philosophers of India, whom
he called *Kalanoi*. The *Kalanoi* in their turn were descended
from the Persian *magi* (fr. 5–13 Wehrli). Oriental wisdom
was thus unified in a genealogical tree in which the Jews
were the descendants of the Persian wise men. Clearchus
wrote a dialogue on sleep, in which he introduced his master
Aristotle as the main speaker. Aristotle was made to report
what was obviously an imaginary conversation with a
Jewish sage whom he supposedly met somewhere in Asia
Minor. The Jew had left Judaea, where the capital has a
name difficult to pronounce (they call it Ierusalem) and had
come down to the sea. He had visited many nations and was
a Greek not only in language, but in soul. Having talked to
so many sages, he was able to instruct Aristotle. What his
wisdom was about we are not told directly; but Hans Lewy
(*Harv. Theol. Rev.* 31 (1938), 205–36) argued plausibly
that it was about experiments in induced lethargy (as after

85

all the title of Clearchus' dialogue about sleep suggests). Such experiments had a bearing on the problem of the nature of the human soul. We now know a little more about Clearchus of Soli, thanks to an unusual inscription which was recently published and admirably illustrated by Louis Robert. In the French excavations at Ai Khanoum in Afghanistan an inscription was found with a series of sentences of Delphic wisdom. An introductory epigram states that Clearchus copied them exactly in Delphi and brought them to this remote place of Bactriana. There seems to be little doubt that Robert is right in identifying this Clearchus with the pupil of Aristotle (*C. R. Acad. Inscr.* (1968), 416–57). This means that he travelled widely and explored the East in which he was interested.

The picture is consistent. In the first thirty or forty years after the destruction of the Persian Empire, Greek philosophers and historians discovered the Jews. They depicted them – both in fact and in fiction – as priestly sages of the type the East was expected to produce. The writers were important and responsible persons. They certainly meant to impress the Greek readers with the wisdom of the Jews. They probably expected to have Jewish readers too. We have no way of measuring the immediate impact of this writing on Jewish readers because we have no document we can safely date about 300 B.C. But if it is true that Kohelet, Ecclesiastes, wrote in the early third century B.C., one must acknowledge that at least one of the Jewish sages was not prepared to play the part the Greeks had assigned to him. Whatever may be said about Ecclesiastes – and many things have been said about him – he decried traditional wisdom. He was certainly a God-fearing man but the God of his fathers was above him, not with him – exactly the opposite position to that of Spinoza. He saw little sense in life. He had nothing of the self-assurance the Greeks liked to attribute to wise Jewish men. At the other end of the social scale Moschos, the son of Moschion, the Jewish slave, has now emerged from a most improbable place – from the temple of Amphiaraus in Boeotia. Anxious about his prospects of liberation, the slave Moschos went for a night of incubation to the temple and had a dream in which the divine pair Amphiaraus and Hygieia ordered him to write down what he had seen and to set it up in stone by the altar. This inscription must be roughly contemporary with Kohelet – that is, not later than 250 B.C. 'The first Greek Jew', as David Lewis called him (*Journ. Semit. Studies* 2 (1957), 264–6), shows himself as a frightened little being who had been sold into slavery in a remote land. He had not forgotten that he was a Jew, but had recognized the power of the gods of his masters and had acted in accordance with their orders. He was not ready for the role of the philosopher-priest either.

III

Behind Kohelet and Moschos the world had moved fast, and what was already at the start a semi-Utopian picture by Greek philosophers soon became absurd.

More and more Greeks and Macedonians moved into Palestine, either on royal initiative or by choice: they encouraged the Hellenization of the natives. Greek cities developed, especially along the Mediterranean coast and near the Sea of Tiberias. Some of the cities – such as Acco, Dor, Jaffa, Ascalon, Gaza, Pella, Philadelpheia, Scythopolis, Samaria – were ancient towns which changed style and occasionally names: Philadelpheia is the new name for Rabbat-Ammon; Scythopolis for Bet-Shean. The Greek cities were fortresses, markets and intellectual centres. Saul Weinberg's exploration at Tel Anafa in Upper Galilee is now beginning to give us an idea of a small Hellenistic centre of the second century B.C. in its intercourse with Phoenician towns and with the Greek world of the eastern Mediterranean. Menippus, the Greek counterpart of Kohelet, came from Gadara in Transjordan; he was Hellenized rather than Greek. The same applies to his later fellow-citizens Meleager, the subtle writer of epigrams, and Philodemus the Epicurean. Meleager was very conscious of his Semitic origins. From his imaginary tomb he greeted the passer-by trilingually: 'If you are a Syrian, Salam; if you are a Phoenician, Naidios [the word is certainly corrupt]; if you are a Greek, Chaire; and say the same yourself' (*Anth. Gr.* 7.419). One of Meleager's rivals in love was a Jew, and Meleager commented with resignation: 'Love burns hot even on cold Sabbaths' (5.160). This is the idyllic part of a transformation which had far harsher sides. As the events of the second century were to show, Jews and Gentiles could be beastly to each other on Palestinian soil.

In the third century B.C. Judaea proper was a small part of Palestine: it was almost identifiable with the territory of the city of Jerusalem, and as such it was still envisaged by Polybius in the middle of the second century B.C. (16, fr. 39). Samaria and Galilee were outside it. The Samaritans – or at least those of them who were not entirely Hellenized – had built up a religious centre of their own on Mount Garizim in circumstances which contradictory legends have rendered unrecognizable. A council of laymen and priests under the presidency of the High Priest had a large measure of autonomy in its government of Jerusalem, but the presence of Ptolemaic garrisons in the country must be assumed. The Zenon Papyri have shown how in about 259 B.C. the agents of the finance minister Apollonius operated in the interests of their master: one of his estates was at Bet Anat in Galilee (*Corpus Papyrorum Judaicarum* 1, 1–5). From the same papyri we learn that the Ptolemies had picked up the well-known Sheikh of Transjordan, Tobiah, to command the military settlers in his territory. Tobiah was a Jew by religion but had his own temple on his own land – and nobody seems to have questioned his orthodoxy. One of his ancestors was Tobiah 'the Ammonite slave' who gave trouble to Nehemiah (Neh. 2.10; 13.4). One of his sons, Joseph, became the chief tax-collector for Judaea about 230 B.C. (Jos. *Ant. Jud.* 12.160 ff.). The High Priest and his council had to reckon with the Tobiads. They were not in a position to remind them that 'an Ammonite and a Moabite shall not enter the congregation of the Lord' (Deut. 23.4) – if it is true that the Tobiads were Ammonites. The slave trade was as rampant as ever, and Ptolemy Philadelphus had to intervene to prohibit attempts at enslaving the free people of Palestine (*Sammelbuch* 8008).

The pressures of the new society were equally manifest in the emigration of Jews from Judaea. Here again compulsion and free choice combined. Egypt was a traditional and obvious place for needy Jews to go. The basic figures we have for this emigration – 100,000 prisoners of war brought from Palestine into Egypt by Ptolemy I (*Aristeas* 12–14) and 1,000,000 Jews in Egypt at the time of Philo (*in Flacc.* 43) – are almost certainly both false. Jews went into Egypt to exercise the old professions at which they were good – they were soldiers, tillers, shepherds. The transition from soldier to peasant and vice versa was normal. The strongly centralized administration gave Jews opportunities to enter the king's service as policemen and tax-collectors; foreigners were preferred in such posts. Papyri are less informative about economic life in Alexandria. We know therefore less about Jews as artisans, traders and bankers in the city; but they existed. The Third Book of Maccabees (3.10) has a reference to Greeks who were business partners of Jews in Alexandria about the end of the third century. Egypt was probably the point of departure for further emigration to Cyrene, to Greece and to Italy. There were Jewish communities of some size in Sicyon, Sparta, Delos, Cos and Rhodes in the second part of the second century B.C. In 139 B.C. Jews were thrown out of Rome for obnoxious religious propaganda (Valerius Maximus 1.3.3). The creation of a vast diaspora favoured the priestly class in Jerusalem, as it increased the number of those who paid tribute to the Temple. Pilgrimages to Jerusalem became a much more solemn and expensive occasion. But the description of these pilgrimages in Philo (*De spec. Leg.* 1.69), in the Acts of the Apostles 2.5–11) and in Josephus clearly reflects the later conditions of the *pax romana*, and the commercialization of religious devotion by Herodes.

The figure of 2,700,000 pilgrims per year, which is given by Josephus (*Bellum Jud.* 6.9.3), is another of those impossible data with which the historian of antiquity has to learn to live. Even on a far smaller scale the pilgrimages to Jerusalem of the third century B.C. must have represented important events. They provided a meeting point for people who were increasingly diversified in language, manners, status and even political allegiance. The Babylonian Jews were loyal to the Seleucids; 8,000 of them fought off an attack of marauding Galatians, according to the Second Book of Maccabees (8.20). Louis Finkelstein has shown to my satisfaction – but not, I must admit, to everybody's satisfaction – that the Midrash of the Passover Haggadah reflects these conflicts of political allegiance. Legends about the Babylonian and Persian period were revived – or perhaps invented for the first time – to encourage faithfulness to the Mosaic Law in the new conditions. The first part of the Book of Daniel (approximately chapters 1–6) and the Books of Esther and Judith are more likely to belong to the third than to the second century B.C. They combine edification with entertainment. They show concern for the preservation of the Law, but no pressing anxiety. There is not in them that sombre atmosphere of a mortal struggle which we find in the second part of Daniel.

The fact that the Mediterranean diaspora had rapidly become Greek posed a problem about the knowledge of the Torah. In Palestine and Babylonia Hebrew had remained a literary language. Oral translation of the Bible into Aramaic was sufficient to keep the ignorant informed. In Egypt knowledge of Hebrew became exceptional, while there were all the attractions of Greek literature. The Torah had to be made accessible in Greek both for religious service and for private reading. That meant a written translation. From the Torah the translation was later extended to the rest of the Bible. The process may have taken two centuries. The Book of Esther was probably translated only in 78/77 B.C.

The translation must also have helped proselytism, which acquired quite different dimensions as soon as the Jews began to speak Greek. I do not know of any Hellenistic evidence to show that a Gentile became a Jew or a sympathizer because he had read the Bible. But Philo says that many Gentiles – that is, I presume, sympathizers – took part in the annual festival on the island of Pharos to celebrate the translation of the LXX (*Vita Mosis* 2.41). The sacred books had become accessible to those who were interested in Judaism. There is, however, no sign that the Gentiles at large ever became acquainted with the Bible: it was bad Greek. No Hellenistic poet or philosopher quoted it, although modern scholars have sometimes deluded themselves on this subject. The first certain quotation of the Bible in a Greek philosopher is to be found in the treatise *On the Sublime* attributed to Longinus which is usually dated in the first century A.D. (9.8). Behind it there is probably the teaching of the rhetorician Caecilius of Calacte, who was a Jew. It is the parochial character of the LXX – its obvious derivation from the methods of oral translation in the Synagogue – which makes it improbable that it should have been translated by command of Ptolemy II. I never disagree lightly with Elias Bickerman who has defended this tradition, already current in the second century B.C. – only one century after the alleged event. Bickerman argued that in antiquity big enterprises of translation were due to public, not private, initiative. But he could quote only the case of the thirty books on agriculture by the Carthaginian Mago which were translated into Latin by order of the Roman Senate (Pliny, *N.H.* 18.22). The Romans had a different attitude to translations from that of the Greeks. In the third century B.C. Livius Andronicus was brought to Rome to be a semi-official translator of Greek poetry into Latin. In the absence of anything comparable among the Greeks, I hesitate to attribute to royal initiative a translation so clearly born within the

precincts of the synagogue. The LXX remained an exclusive
Jewish possession until the Christians took it over. We do not
even know whether it was deposited in that great Ptolemaic
foundation, the library of Alexandria.

The consequence must now be faced. About 300 B.C.
Greek intellectuals presented the Jews to the Greek world
as philosophers, legislators and wise men. A few decades
later, the alleged philosophers and legislators made public in
Greek their own philosophy and legislation. The Gentile
world remained indifferent. Other Semites, the Phoenician
Zeno of Citium and Chrysippus of Soli, came to Athens and
easily established themselves as masters of wisdom in the
very centre of intellectual life in Greece, because they
accepted polytheism and made the traditional language of
Greek philosophy their own. The contrast was glaring. The
failure of the LXX to arouse the interest of the pagan intel-
ligentsia of the third century B.C. was the end of the myth
of the Jewish philosopher.

Let us consider more closely what was implied in the
Greek refusal to look at the Bible. It meant that the Greeks
expected the Jews not to translate their holy books, but to
produce an account of themselves according to the current
methods and categories of ethnography. This was an old
practice in the Greek world. In the fifth century B.C.
Xanthus of Lydia had written in Greek a book on Lydian
history and customs which was probably inspired by Herodotus. In the third century books of this kind were multi-
plying. The Egyptian Manetho, the Babylonian Berossus
and the Roman Fabius Pictor wrote the histories of their
respective countries in a suitable version for the benefit of
the Greeks. It was easy for the Jews to comply with this
custom because Hecataeus of Abdera had produced a little
model of what was expected of them. Thus, in a sense, the
Jews were asked to perpetuate their own myth in the terms
in which the Greeks had invented it. Some Jews obliged. We
know that a Demetrius (whom Flavius Josephus foolishly
calls Demetrius of Phalerum) composed a biblical history,

including the chronological enquiries which were fashionable. This must have happened in the late third century. Not much later a man who was probably a Samaritan composed another history of biblical times. But the most famous of such treatises about the Jews were written in the middle of the second century. Eupolemus, who was Judas Maccabaeus' envoy to Rome in 161 B.C., composed a work in which one could read an exchange of letters between the twelve-year-old Solomon and his client kings Vaphres of Egypt and Suron of Tyre (Eusebius, *Praep. Evang.* 9.31–4). Another historian, the very mysterious Malchus or Cleodemus, whose Jewish origin is only probable, presented the sons of Abraham as companions of Hercules who married the daughter of one of them (Jos. *Ant. Jud.* 1.240). Aristobulus of Paneas allegorized Hebrew tradition in a dialogue in which Ptolemy VI (181–145 B.C.) asked questions about the Bible. This approach made it inherently possible for the Jews to claim to have been the teachers of the Greeks owing to their own greater antiquity. About 200 B.C. the biographer Hermippus accepted without difficulty the notion that Pythagoras had been a pupil of Jews and Thracians. The Jews were also entitled to seek respectable genealogical connections with the Greeks. Somebody – either Jew or Greek – invented a common descent of Jews and Spartans from Abraham. It is apparent from the Second Book of Maccabees that at least some Jewish circles admitted the claim – which had many parallels in the Hellenistic world. It was also established that the Jews had been friends of the inhabitants of Pergamum in the time of Abraham (*Ant. Jud.* 14.255). Indeed, Abraham, more cosmopolitan and less legalistic than Moses, became the favourite hero of such concoctions.

All this was not only demoralizing. It was positively dangerous because it involved the Jews in a game in which they were bound to be discredited. The game, as I have indicated, was played in an atmosphere of mounting tensions. In Palestine the Jews had to face the intruding Greeks.

93

In Egypt they were the intruders. In the third century B.C. they were still co-operating with the Greeks in Egypt, but they were becoming unpopular with the natives. Two theories about the Jews circulated under the name of Manetho. One identified them with the invading Hyksos, the other with lepers. It is a famous question whether the well-deserving historian Manetho was responsible for either of these theories. The Jews defended themselves by quoting Hecataeus of Abdera. Here again it is a famous question whether what Flavius Josephus and Eusebius quote under the name of Hecataeus is authentic. Hans Lewy is another scholar with whom one can disagree only at one's peril, and Hans Lewy maintained in an admirable paper that at least what Josephus quotes is authentic Hecataeus. I am, however, inclined to believe that the authentic Hecataeus could not have stated, as Josephus makes him state, that Alexander gave the Samaritan territory free of tax to the Jews. Whether authentic or not, this material from Manetho and Hecataeus was used for mean purposes of reciprocal abuse. Forgeries of Greek poetry completed this work.

The worst was still to come. In the second century the religious and social conflicts became far more acute. When Palestine was turned into Syrian territory in 198, it was soon involved in the process of decomposition of the Hellenistic system under Roman pressure. In Egypt the Jews had to take sides in the hostilities between the various factions which competed for whatever power was left under the virtual protectorate of Rome. Accusations of ritual murder and of anti-Greek oaths were levelled against the Jews. Somebody insinuated that the Jews worshipped a donkey's head in their Temple. The story goes back to Mnaseas, a writer of the second half of the second century B.C. (*c. Apionem* 2.112). It became widely known through the book written against the Jews by Apollonius Molon, one of Cicero's teachers.

It is not my purpose to follow up in detail the story of the literary abuse which accompanied and followed the

Maccabean rebellion and the much less glorious establishment of the Hasmonean dynasty. I shall, however, discuss
the tradition about the Maccabees in my next lecture. What
is clear is that with the elimination of the only authentic
document – the Bible – from the picture, the discussion was
bound to degenerate. The philosophers were not allowed
to produce their philosophy. The *Ersatz* they were asked to
give, and gave, was of low quality.

While peace still lasted, but with some expectation of
trouble to come, Simon ben Jesus ben Eleazar ben Sira, as
he was apparently called, wrote his meditations – the
Ecclesiasticus. They must belong to the period 190–170 B.C.
Ben Sira had wandered abroad (51.13), and his ideal scribe
was a man who had travelled 'through the lands of the
peoples' and had tested 'good and evil among men' (39.4). I
do not see any clear trace that Ben Sira had read Greek
books, and I do not believe that he needed the *Iliad* to learn
that men 'sprout and fade like leaves of a tree' (14.18). But
he had certainly seen something of the Greek civilization,
with its philosophic schools, theatres and gymnasia. He fore-
saw a war and prayed for the victory of his people. He also
saw social antagonisms growing in Palestine and advised
charity and justice. But he had really no message, either for
victory or for reform. His book, steeped as it was in the Pro-
verbs and in the Psalms, quietly reaffirmed Jewish traditional
faith against the temptations of Hellenism: 'Fear God with
all your heart and reverence his priests' (7.29). Ben Sira
praised the fathers of old and described the High Priest
Simon son of Jochanan in his majestic appearance when he
went up to the altar (50.11). He concluded (if this is the
correct reading) 'May my soul delight in my Yeshibah'
(51.29).

As a personal evaluation of a hundred years of Jewish-
Greek contacts this was a remarkable statement. It was a
return to the Bible by a scribe who had seen the consequences
of Hellenization. By writing in Hebrew and preserving their
spiritual independence, men like Kohelet and Ben Sira

saved the Jews from the intellectual sterility which characterized Egyptian and Babylonian life under the Hellenistic
kings. The Romans, too, avoided total absorption in Hellenistic modes of thought, but after all they were politically
independent and soon became more powerful than any
Hellenistic kingdom. The Jews remained alive by sheer
obstinacy of faith. There is, however, another side of the
story – and this will be our end for today. The Hebrew text
of Ben Sira, which accompanied the sectarians of Qumran
and the defenders of Masada, was lost in the early Middle
Ages and was only partially recovered in the Cairo *Geniza*
at the end of the last century. The book by the man who had
repudiated Greek wisdom lived on through the centuries in
the Greek version made by his grandson – an émigré to
Egypt in 132 B.C.

5

Greeks, Jews and Romans from
Antiochus III to Pompey

I

'It is unlawful for any foreigner to enter the enclosure of the
temple which is forbidden to the Jews, except to those of
them who are accustomed to enter after purifying themselves in accordance with the law of the country. Nor shall
anyone bring into the city the flesh of horses or of mules or
of wild or tame asses, or of leopards, foxes or hares or, in
general, of any animals forbidden to the Jews.' This is not
a piece of the Mishnaic treatise *Kelim*: it is a decree of
Antiochus III, King of Syria, enacted about 200 B.C. (Joseph.
Antiq. Jud. 12.145–6), and its authenticity has been proved
beyond any doubt by Elias Bickerman, the scholar who,
more than any other, has taught us to understand Judaism
in its Hellenistic surroundings (*Syria* 25 (1946–8), 67–85).
Suddenly, after two centuries of obscurity and legends, two
documents coming from the chancery of Antiochus III
allow us to see something of the life of Jerusalem; the second
document is again quoted by Flavius Josephus (*Ant. Jud.*
12.138–44), and was again defended against doubts of forgery by E. Bickerman, *Rev. Étud. Juives* 100 (1935), 4–35.
What we see is a little temple-state, the economic and social
structures of which had been shattered by the recent wars
between Antiochus III and Ptolemy V. Palestine had passed
from Egyptian to Syrian control. As the Jews were themselves divided in their sympathies and interests, the pro-
Egyptian leaders had to take refuge in Egypt (Hieron. *in*

Dan. 11.14; *P.L.* 25.562). Many other Jews had been enslaved or had run away. The finances and even the buildings
of the Temple were damaged. In recognition of the support
which the majority of the Jewish aristocracy had given him,
Antiochus III tried to help his new subjects. In a letter to the
local governor, Ptolemy, whom we know from another text
(*OGIS* 230), Antiochus III grants various tax exemptions
and subsidies to the Jewish population of Judaea and especially to their 'senate, priests, scribes and sacred singers'.
Interestingly enough, the High Priest is not mentioned in
any form in these documents: yet he was the Simon whom
Ben Sira described in his encomium as a restorer of the
fortunes of Jerusalem, among other things. The king of
Syria sees Judaea as a city-state, however peculiar, with its
senate and other well-defined corporations, priests, scribes,
singers. The main fact which emerges is that the Temple is
still being subsidized by the king of the land, as it was under
Persian rule, according to a decree of Darius of 515 B.C.
(Ezra 6.9). It seems fairly certain that this subvention, which
Artaxerxes I had confirmed in 459 B.C. (Ezra 7.21–2), had
been continued by Alexander and the Ptolemies: it was
later reconfirmed, though with a changed formula, by
Augustus (Phil. *Leg. ad Gaium* 157; Jos. *B.J.* 2.409). The
economy of the Temple, and with it the Jewish cult, depended on the goodwill of the suzerain. Antiochus III fixed this
subsidy at 20,000 silver drachmae plus a contribution in
kind of corn and salt. What proportion of the total expenses
of the Temple this subsidy represented we do not know,
but it was certainly very substantial. The price the Jews were
expected to pay for this help was co-operation and conformity. A disagreement between the high priest and the
royal supervisor of the Temple under Seleucus IV about 180
resulted in an inspection by the Visir Heliodorus, another
personality well known from other evidence (*OGIS* 247).
We all remember what happened. Like the Persian Datis at
the temple of Athena Lindia on the island of Rhodes (*Inscr.
Lindos* 1, 183–4 Blinkenberg), Heliodorus was stopped by

Greeks, Jews and Romans

miracles and compelled to admit the presence of a great god. The miracles, which were no doubt immediately registered by a contemporary aretology, were later collected and conflated by the source of II Maccabees before the end of the second century B.C. As nobody was interested in such a small episode after the Maccabean rebellion, we have here the authentic voice of priestly Jerusalem before the revolutionary period. Like the decrees by Antiochus III, the aretology concerning Heliodorus is a survival of the well-mannered days in which the Seleucids subsidized the Jewish Temple and backed out in good or bad order if they encountered resistance. No serious issue was yet in sight.

How the serious issues emerged within a few years of the miracle of Heliodorus is the question. Certain facts belong to general Hellenistic history. The Jews were caught in the war between Antiochus IV Epiphanes and Ptolemy VI Philometor in which Egypt was saved by Roman intervention in 168 B.C. Antiochus IV who was robbed of his victory by the Romans tried to cope with the consequent social and economic problems by interfering with indigenous sanctuaries and their finances. He was interested in reinforcing the life of the Greek cities and extending the Hellenization of his subjects. His unpredictable character, which was noticed by Polybius (26.1), was in itself an element of the situation. Problems of Hellenization of course existed everywhere. While in Judaea the compiler of the Book of Daniel was adapting to the situation the old image of the Fourth Kingdom, part iron and part clay (D. Flusser, *Israel Oriental Studies* 2 (1972), 148–75), Cato was making jokes in Rome against the Greeks. A generation later Cicero's grandfather, 'vir optimus', was certain that knowledge of Greek was a mark of iniquity: 'ut quisque optime Graece sciret, ita esse nequissimum' (*De orat.* 2.265). Only our deplorable ignorance of Carthaginian and Parthian jokes prevents us from assessing the local reactions to 'pergraecari', a word which Festus explains as 'epulis et potationibus inservire' (p. 235 L.).

99

But what happened in Jerusalem between 168 and 164
B.C. went beyond the ordinary internal conflicts of the
Seleucid state. The Temple of Yahwe was turned into a
temple of Zeus Olympios, the inhabitants of Jerusalem were
called Antiochenes and the mysterious Acra, the fortress,
was occupied by a Syrian garrison: traditional Jewish practices, such as circumcision and the observance of the Sabbath, were prohibited. Such direct interference in the
ancestral cults of a nation was unheard of in the Greek-
speaking world from immemorial times. At least a section
of the Jews felt that the only answer was a holy war. Judas
the Maccabee emerged as the new leader of the nation.
Within three years, probably about December (Kislev) 164,
the ancestral cult was re-established in the Temple. Yet a
return to the ordinary relations between a temple-state and
the Seleucid sovereign was out of the question. There were
too many pretenders to the weak Syrian throne for such a
return to be feasible. Politically, the Maccabean rebellion
soon became a war for independence. As independence was
possible only with Roman help and authorization, independence in fact meant turning Judaea into a vassal state of
Rome. The first step in that direction was taken by Judas
in 161 B.C., when he made his treaty of alliance with the
Romans. Culturally, the Palestinian Jews had to face the
increasing differentiation of the diaspora, both in Mesopotamia and in Egypt; they also had to run a state efficiently
within a Hellenistic milieu. Religiously, the rebellion had
created an antinomy. The repudiation of Hellenism in
Jerusalem was certainly a reassertion of the faithfulness of
the Jewish community to the God of Abraham, Isaac and
Jacob, but it was at the same time the result of many individual choices. Thousands of people had been presented with
an alternative and had decided according to an inner inspiration. Some people, in answering the call, had suffered
martyrdom. Antiochus' persecution and the Seven Brothers'
martyrdom typified the situation. Martyrdom was indeed
the new value of the age. But where there is martyrdom,

there is right to secession. The Qumran monks and later the
Christians derived their strength in nonconformity from
the same sources which Judas the Maccabee had discovered
in the desert of Judaea. The slow tempo of the mutual
exploration and adaptation between Jews and Hellenes was
replaced by a feverish crescendo of conflicts.

II

The question we should like to be able to answer is, therefore, what suddenly created such a new, unheard of, situation
in the religious life of antiquity. The fact that the main
course of events is hardly in dispute conceals our ignorance
of the real process. With the Maccabees we feel on the
threshold of a new epoch, the end of tolerance and the
beginning of persecution, and naturally we want to know
both what brought about this change and how the protagonists saw the events in which they played a part. There
are formidable difficulties in trying to elucidate the situation. The historians of Judaism, or for that matter of
Hellenism, are seldom prepared to admit the full extent of
our ignorance, which is only partly due to the paucity and
contradictions of the evidence. There is an intrinsic difficulty
in understanding even very simple and comparatively well-
documented episodes of religious wars. Twice my bloody
Piedmontese tried to get rid of the Protestants at their gates.
In both cases they failed. In 1602 they were thrown down
from the walls of Geneva which they had assaulted by surprise. In 1689 they could not prevent the warlike return of
the Waldenses to their native valleys. The Escalade and the
Grande Rentrée are respectively for the Calvinists of Geneva
and the Waldenses of Torre Pellice what the reconsecration
of the Temple is to the Jews; and they offer the same problems not only of separating facts from legends, but of grasping the meaning of the facts. Was the pastor Henri Arnaud,
the Judas Maccabaeus of the Waldenses, the *longa manus*
of England? Is such a proposition indeed meaningful?

First of all, we are virtually deprived of the Seleucid, or more generally the Hellenic, version of the events in Judaea. A series of documents both in the First and in the Second Book of Maccabees reflects – I believe quite authentically for the majority of them – the decline of Syrian power in Judaea, but does not offer any precise clue to the intentions of Antiochus IV in Hellenizing Jerusalem. The accounts of Polybius and Posidonius are almost entirely lost. It is perhaps possible to recognize traces of the version of Nicolas of Damascus in the account of Josephus in *Bellum Judaicum* I if we compare it with the much more elaborate story told by Josephus in his *Antiquitates Judaicae*. But if Josephus used Nicolas of Damascus, he reinterpreted him in Jewish terms. The further suggestion that Nicolas of Damascus may in his turn have used Polybius only shows that the subject is not worth pursuing. We are left with no genuine account of the wars between Seleucids and Jews from the Greek point of view. What we have are some rather vague hints in later sources. The most important is of course in Tacitus' excursus on the Jews in the *Histories*. Tacitus takes the view that Antiochus IV tried to improve the Jews by abolishing their superstitions and giving them Greek customs: 'demere superstitionem et mores Graecorum dare adnisus, quo minus taeterrimam gentem in melius mutaret' (5.8). Next in importance is the sixth-century chronicler John Malalas of Antioch (*Chronographia*, 205–7 Dindorf). His story is that the Jews had difficulty in getting corn from Egypt in times of famine, and Antiochus IV made war on Egypt to help his Jewish subjects. But the Jews rebelled after a defeat, and Antiochus IV naturally turned against them, killed all the inhabitants of Jerusalem and converted the Temple into a pagan sanctuary. The story is largely made up of legendary motifs, biblical recollections and Christian hostility; it is after all meant to explain how the Christians took over a Jewish synagogue in Antioch which preserved, according to another source, the mantle of Moses, the surviving fragments of the Law tables, the keys of the Ark and other treasures. Behind John Malalas' tale there is probably a Seleucid version presenting the Jews simply as rebels against the authority of Antiochus IV, but it is not a version we can use in any responsible way for the reconstruction of the events (E. Bickerman, *Byzantion* 21 (1951), 63–83).

III

There is of course abundant Jewish evidence. Yet, in my opinion, the only two continuous accounts of the events – the First and Second Books of Maccabees – cannot be taken as contemporary witnesses to the facts. The style of the First Book of Maccabees betrays itself as a translation from a Hebrew text: St Jerome apparently still saw the Hebrew original (*Div. Biblioth.*, *P.L.* 28.556), and Origen still knew its Hebrew title, which has come down to us in a corrupt and unintelligible form, *Sarbethsabanaiel* (ap. Euseb. *H.E.* 6.25.2). The text stops with the death of Simon in 135 and is likely to have been written under his successor John Hyrcanus, that is, before 104. The date of the Greek translation is, strictly speaking, unknown, though a *terminus ante quem* is provided by Flavius Josephus who used it extensively – with the possible exception of the last three chapters (a point that concerns Josephus, but not the integrity of I Maccabees). As the Greek translation is obviously faithful to the Hebrew original the date of the translation is irrelevant to its value as a historical source.

The Second Book of Maccabees presents itself as a summary of a work in five books composed by Jason of Cyrene, otherwise unknown (2.19–28). There is no reason to doubt the correctness of this claim. The epitome begins with two letters. The first letter, from the Jews of Judaea to the Jews of Egypt, commends the celebration of the Feast of the Purification of the Temple and is dated in 124 B.C. The second letter, from Judas Maccabaeus and the people of Jerusalem to Aristobulus, 'teacher of King Ptolemy (Philometor)', is apparently dated in 164 B.C.: it tells the story of the end of Antiochus IV and the institution of the Feast of the Purification of the Temple. The first letter is very probably authentic, the second probably forged and intended to reinforce the first letter. Nothing could impress the Jews of Egypt more favourably than a letter by Judas Maccabaeus in person to the very respected Jewish-Egyptian writer Aristobulus, who will recur in our story. If the epitomist added the two letters to his summary of the history of Jason, his epitome must be dated after 124 B.C. The only possible alternative is the assumption that a later interpolator added the two letters to the epitome of Jason. Though the theory of a third hand – the interpolator of the epitomist of Jason – has been propounded several times – and even recently by Diego Arenhoevel in his excellent book *Die Theokratie nach dem I. und II. Makkabäerbuch* – I have never found it supported by sufficient evidence.

I know of only one serious reason for suspecting interpolations in the present text of II Maccabees. This is the verse 10.1, in which Judas Maccabaeus is called Μακκαβαῖος without the preceding article, whereas in nineteen other passages Μακκαβαῖος is preceded by the article. This linguistic argument is, however, less impressive on closer inspection. The expression in which Μακκαβαῖος appears without the article is Μακκαβαῖος δὲ καὶ οἱ σὺν αὐτῷ, 'Maccabee and his followers', which has no parallel in the other nineteen cases in which Μακκαβαῖος is preceded by the article. The only parallel passage is 8.1 where the text reads Ἰούδας δὲ ὁ καὶ Μακκαβαῖος καὶ οἱ σὺν αὐτῷ, 'Judas the Maccabee and his followers'. Here the name Ἰούδας is without article, just as Μακκαβαῖος is without article in 10.1. I do not know of any thorough research on the usage of the article with personal names in II Maccabees. Pending further research, I cannot consider the word Μακκαβαῖος in 10.1 to be inconsistent with the language of the rest of the book and therefore evidence of interpolation.

The obvious interpretation of the Second Book of Maccabees is that its author was interested in propagating the celebration of the Feast of the Purification of the Temple among Egyptian Jews. He recommended such celebration both by summarizing the history of Jason of Cyrene – who gave an account of the events – and by introducing the two letters of the Palestinian Jews who invited the Egyptian Jews to join in the celebration. The epitomist himself emphasizes that he is writing at a certain distance from the events because he concludes his story with the words: 'From this time Jerusalem has been in the possession of the Jews.' If 124 B.C. is the likely *terminus post quem* for II Maccabees, the *terminus ante quem* is the occupation of Judaea by Pompey. The stress laid on the new Festival of Purification of the Temple favours a date in the late second century B.C. In other words, I am inclined to put both I and II Maccabees in the last decades of the second century B.C., about forty or fifty years after the death of Antiochus IV in 164 B.C. The two main Jewish sources were written when Judaea had become an independent and expansionist state. The very adventurous course of its politics at that time bore little resemblance to the mortal struggle in religious terms of the period of Antiochus IV. We must keep in mind the possibility that the two books reflect a later atmosphere in their accounts of distant events. The First Book of Maccabees is a dynastic history of the Hasmoneans and presents an incoherent and contradictory view of the policy of Antiochus IV. When Antiochus became king certain lawless Jews obtained permission to perform the rites of the heathen in Jerusalem: they forsook circumcision and built gymnasia. Next, however, having invaded Egypt, Antiochus himself sacked the Temple of Jerusalem, occupied the Acra with a garrison and ordered all the peoples in his kingdom to renounce their own laws. At this point of the account Antiochus has become a Hellenizer far beyond Judaea, and the Hellenizing group of Jerusalem has no longer any relevant part in the story. By contrast, II Maccabees centres its story consistently on the misdeeds of the Jewish Hellenizers and on the conflicts between the various Jewish factions. It insists to the last on the existence and activities of opponents to Judas Maccabaeus, including the former High Priest Alcimus. We owe to II Maccabees the information that both the Temple of Jerusalem and the Samaritan temple on Mount Garizim were transformed into Greek temples (of Zeus Olympios and of Zeus Xenios) and that the festival of the Dionysia was celebrated in Jerusalem. II Maccabees is not interested in following up the destiny of the Samaritan temple, which must have indirectly benefited from the rebellion of Judas Maccabaeus.

It is not surprising that the version of II Maccabees should appeal to us as being both more consistent and nearer to our own experience. As is well known, it was made the basis of a reconstruction of the events by V. Tcherikover and E. Bickerman. The existence of a strong Hellenizing party in Jerusalem, which asked for and obtained the support of the Seleucid king, explains what in Hellenistic terms was the exceptional behaviour of Antiochus IV. Furthermore, the analogy of the nineteenth-century movements of assimilation among the Jews – with the establishment of reformed synagogues in the Protestant style – creates a presumption of truth in this version. The existence of a Hellenizing party in Judaea about 170 B.C. can indeed be taken for granted. The question, however, is whether II Maccabees does not present a gross simplification of events which prompts us to misleading analogies. II Maccabees is not a book to be used without some closer scrutiny. It can tell its readers that Antiochus IV, in mortal danger, promised to 'become a Jew and to visit every inhabited place in order to proclaim the power of God' (9.17). We must now turn to the only authentic documents which can be dated between 167 and 164 B.C. and show the progress of the persecution: the petition of the Samaritans of Shechem to Antiochus IV which is reported by Flavius Josephus (*Ant. Jud.* 12.258 ff.) and the Book of Daniel.

IV

I cannot include any Psalm among the certain contemporary documents, because I confess my inability to date any Psalm securely in the Maccabean period. As we have no continuous contemporary account of the persecution of Antiochus IV and of the Maccabean reaction, I do not see how we can decide whether any Psalm may be labelled as Maccabean. There is nothing *a priori* against any of the Psalms belonging to the Maccabean period. The Qumran Psalms Scroll has proved that in the second or even first century B.C. the collection of the Psalms was still open to modifications. But we cannot expect any Psalm reflecting the years of oppression and revolt to be exactly comparable with the situation described from a later point of view in the Books of Maccabees; and if we cannot use the Books of Maccabees in this way any certain terms of comparison are lacking altogether. For example, one of the strongest candidates as a Maccabean Psalm has always been 74: 'O God, why dost thou cast us off for ever? Why doth thine anger smoke against the sheep of thy pasture? Remember thy congregation, which thou hast purchased of old.' The situation here presupposed is a sanctuary on fire, with perpetual ruins and heathen symbols. As the Psalmist does not mention the destruction of the city or the deportation of the people, the context can hardly be the destruction of Jerusalem in 586 B.C. But the description does not correspond either to what we are told in the Books of Maccabees about the defilement of the Temple in 167 B.C., when only the priests' chamber was destroyed and only the gates burned (I Mac. 4.38; II Mac. 1.8; 8.33) – whereas the great event, not mentioned in the Psalm, was 'the abomination of desolation upon the altar'. In the fifth century A.D. Theodoretus felt the difficulty when, in his admirable analysis, he saw in this Psalm a prophecy of the burning of the Temple by Titus (*P.G.* 80.1453). Either the Psalm gives a very different version of the events of 167 or it refers to some other trouble which has left no trace in our tradition, for instance during the wars of the successors of Alexander at the end of the fourth century.

We are therefore left with only two certain pieces of contemporary evidence for the religious situation of the persecution period – as I have said, the Book of Daniel and the petition of the Samaritans of Shechem who wanted to dedicate their temple to Zeus, and more precisely to Zeus Hellenios (Jos. *Ant. Jud.* 12.258 ff.). The Samaritans petitioned the Syrian king in order to dissociate themselves from the Jews, to be considered Sidonians and to give to their god the name of Zeus Hellenios: 'Now you have dealt with the Jews as their wickedness deserves, but the King's officers, in the belief that we follow the same practices as they through kinship with them, are involving us in similar charges, whereas we are Sidonians by origin, as is evident from our state documents. We therefore petition you as our benefactor and saviour to command Apollonius the governor of the district not to molest us in any way, since we are distinct from them both in race and customs ... and we ask that the temple without a name be known as that of Zeus Hellenios' (*Ant. Jud.* 12.260 ff.). This text confirms certain aspects of the situation described by II Maccabees. Just as the Temple of Jerusalem was renamed after Olympian Zeus, the sanctuary on Mount Garizim was to be called after Zeus Xenios (6.1–2). The Samaritans wanted to be treated as Sidonians, just as the inhabitants of Jerusalem were now treated as Antiochenes. I cannot accept M. Delcor's theory that these Sidonians of Sechem were real Phoenicians, not Samaritans (*Zeitschr. Deutsch. Palästina-Ver.* 78 (1962), 2, 4–48). It is not worth discussing the difference between the document of Josephus and II Maccabees over the name which the Samaritan temple was going to take: Zeus Hellenios according to one source, Zeus Xenios according to the other. What the Samaritan document adds to II Maccabees is that the Samaritans petitioned the king for the name of their temple. Not only is there no evidence that the inhabitants of Jerusalem did the same, but the petition of the Samaritans clearly implies that they did not do so. The Samaritan move was an attempt to forestall the king and to avoid the extension of the anti-Jewish measures to the Samaritans. Far from being modelled on a petition by Jerusalem Hellenizers, the Samaritan petition precludes the existence of a Jewish model. To make the point more sharply, the Samaritan document invalidates the theory that Jewish Hellenizers had the decisive word in persuading Antiochus IV to transform the Temple of Jerusalem into a temple of Zeus Olympios.

This conclusion is confirmed by the Book of Daniel. The Book of Daniel, as we have it, devotes its second half – that is, chapters 7–12 in the Hebrew Bible – to visions in which Antiochus IV is easily recognizable. In the vision of the Four Beasts in chapter 7, Antiochus 'changes the seasons and the law' and his rule will last 'a time and times and half a time' (7.25): perhaps three years and a half. Chapter 8 reveals that the desecration of the Temple will last two thousand and three hundred evenings and mornings (8.14), which may be interpreted either as 2,300 days or 1,150 days. As the Temple was desecrated, according to the most probable chronology, about December 167 and reconsecrated about December 164, we must take it that the correct interpretation of Daniel is the latter, amounting to about three years, which is in rough agreement with the 'time, times and half a time' of the previous chapter. The beautiful chapter 9 is much more difficult from the point of view of chronological speculations, because it is a reinterpretation of Jeremiah's 'seventy years for the desolations of Jerusalem' (9.2): but in 9.27 there seems to be a reaffirmation of the period of three and a half years for the suspension of the Temple service. Finally, the time of persecution is stated again to be 'a time, times and half a time' (12.7), that is three years and a half, in the vision of the two angels which concludes the book. The prediction is made more precise by making it equal to 1,290 days and then adding another 45 days (12.11–12) – to the despair of the modern interpreter, but probably to the complete satisfaction of the contemporary reader who read the prophecy just when it had been fulfilled. At the risk of being treated as a terrible simplifier I venture to assert that the author of Daniel 7–12 was evidently writing or at least putting the last touches to his prophecies immediately after the reconsecration of the Temple (in December 164?). He did not yet know, as we know now thanks to the cuneiform tablet B.M. 35603, that Antiochus IV had died in Persia a few days or weeks before the probable date of the reconsecration of the Temple (A. J. Sachs and D. J. Wiseman, *Iraq* 16 (1954), 212). In his only attempt at an authentic prophecy the author of Daniel – or at least of its second half – predicted that Antiochus IV would go to his death in a new war against Egypt – and more precisely 'between the seas and the beauteous holy mountain' (11.45), that is, between the Mediterranean and Jerusalem. That did not happen. As a prophet Daniel had his limitations. Though he knew about the intervention of Rome in 168 B.C. which saved Egypt from conquest by Syria, he prophesied another war between Egypt and Syria, as if the Romans would not again have intervened. He was so absorbed in the rivalry between Egypt and Syria that he attributed comparatively little importance to the fact that the Seleucid monarchy still had a large interest in the Iranian plateau (see, however, 8.5). All this narrowed the horizon of his visions. But within his own terms of reference he was well informed and attentive. He had the knowledge of the dynastic relations between Seleucids and Ptolemies which was necessary for a Jewish observer. What is characteristic of his interpretation is that he did not attribute any importance to the Maccabean movement. There may be an allusion to it in 11.34 'now when they shall stumble, they shall be helped with a little help, but many shall join themselves unto them with blandishments'. In this case, he plays down Judas and his followers as 'a little help', and even suggests that some of these followers had joined the ranks not because they believed in their cause, but under false pretences. Daniel certainly admits the presence of a Hellenizing party. The confession of sins in chapter 9, though conceived in traditional terms, must have a meaning for the present. In chapter 9.27 there may even be an allusion to an agreement between Antiochus and the Hellenizers ('and he shall make a firm covenant with many for one week'). But the impression an impartial reader of Daniel receives is that he attributes no more importance to the Hellenizers than he does to their rivals, the followers of Judas Maccabaeus. He sees Jerusalem in the context of the struggle between Syria and Egypt and more generally within the framework of the kingdoms originating from the conquests of Alexander. The present struggle between Egypt and Syria is assuming in his eyes apocalyptic proportions. Syria, or rather Antiochus, pollutes the Temple of Jerusalem on the eve of a final war which will give him victory over Egypt, but which will soon be followed by the deliverance of the Jews and by the Last Judgement: 'And many of them that sleep in the dust of the earth shall awake, some to everlasting life and some to reproaches and everlasting abhorrence' (12.2).

It is of course very difficult for us to reconcile ourselves to such a perspective. But we must emphasize that Daniel is the only piece of contemporary evidence from the Jewish side: it gives us what at least one Jew thought the situation to be about 164 B.C., immediately after the reconsecration of the Temple but before the death of Antiochus IV was known. It is not the perspective of a man who is dominated by the fear and hatred of Hellenizers. There is a foreign rule which brought contamination with it: the contamination is over and the Last Judgement is in sight. Admittedly, the theology of the end of days is vague enough: Daniel does not seem to expect a universal resurrection of the dead.

The Book of Daniel tells us something about the inner vision which inspired the enemies of Antiochus IV in facing battle and martyrdom. Nor is the Book of Daniel necessarily alone in this perspective. If chapter 90 of the Ethiopic Enoch was written before the death of Judas Maccabaeus, as seems likely, it contains a comparable message. God himself sets up a new Jerusalem, and a Messiah-like figure appears at the end, 'the lamb which became a great animal and had great black horns on its head'. The Book of Jubilees, if written about 120 B.C., confirms the Messianic expectations of that time. I and II Maccabees lost the apocalyptic sense of the struggle. But resurrection to a Messianic Kingdom is surely implied in the words of the mother of the Seven Martyrs in II Maccabees: 'Fear not this executioner, but proving thyself worthy of thy brethren, accept thy death that in the mercy of God I may receive thee again with thy brethren.' Thus the Book of Daniel provides the first intimation of that apocalyptic interpretation of contemporary struggles which was to become an ordinary feature of the later rebellions of the Jews against foreign rule. Messiahs appeared, as we all know, under the procuratorships of Cuspius Fadus and Antonius Felix, and Josephus decried them as men who deceived and deluded the people by their pretence of having received from God in the wilderness the signs of liberty (Jos. *Ant. Jud.* 20.97 ff. and 20.167 ff.; *Bell. Jud.* 2.258 ff.). The Qumran Scroll about the War between the Sons of Light and the Sons of Darkness – whatever its date and purpose – is the most idiosyncratic formulation of this kind of apocalyptic interpretation of a political situation. Later IV Ezra, which was written about A.D. 100, contained visions of the Messianic age in the same context of the anti-Roman struggle. Many rabbis expected a Messiah after the destruction of the Second Temple, and the greatest of them, Rabbi Akiva, found his Messiah in Bar Kochba under Hadrian, though it is very doubtful whether Bar Kochba himself even claimed Messianic status. After Bar Kochba the rabbis had good reason to become suspicious of any apocalyptic movement in Judaism. But we can now see that the apocalyptic interpretation of history emerged from the confrontation with the Greeks about 165 B.C. If II Maccabees reveals a true aspect of the activities of Antiochus IV by stressing the co-operation of Hellenizing Jews, this is something less than the whole truth.

V

But the end of the world does not happen every time people expect it. The Jews had to face the world as it was, and the world was one in which Greek customs prevailed and Roman proconsuls made the law. By trying to combine a theocratic rule in the old Jewish style with a principality on the Hellenistic model, the Hasmoneans found themselves involved in more than ordinary difficulties and contradictions. They tried to enlarge the territory of their state, which was perhaps essential if they were to survive. But they felt unable to admit Gentiles as subjects and therefore embarked on a policy of forced conversions which ultimately resulted in the rise of the poorly Judaized Idumean Herodes to the throne of Jerusalem. While a broad toleration of different opinions characterized Jewish religious thought as such during the first century B.C. the conflicts between political and religious leaders, especially of the Pharisaic persuasion, were murderous. The diplomatic game required knowledge of Greek style and observance of Greek conventions. The first Jewish embassy to Rome under Judas Maccabaeus appears to have included the historian Eupolemus, who wrote a history of the Jews in Greek and maintained that the Phoenicians and consequently the Greeks had learnt the art of writing from Moses (cf. I Mac. 8.17).

The family link between the Jews and the Spartans was not invented by the Hasmoneans. Compelled to flee from Jerusalem about 168, the High Priest Jason chose to go to Sparta, evidently because the legend of the Spartans being relatives of the Jews had already acquired currency (II Mac. 5.9). But it fell to the lot of the Hasmoneans to exploit this legend for political respectability. After all the Spartans were said to be relatives of the Sabines who had given many wives and some kings to the Romans. The First Book of the Maccabees quotes a letter from Jonathan the Maccabee to the Spartans which is probably authentic (12.6) and a letter from the Spartans to his successor Simon which is certainly authentic

(14.20). A letter by King Areus of Sparta to the Jews, which would date the discovery of the family connection in the first half of the third century B.C., was probably forged to provide a background for the authentic correspondence of the second century (cf. 12.7).

Some of these diplomatic operations can only have been performed for the gratification of the Jews themselves. I Maccabees contains, as we all know, one of the most re- markable encomia of Rome in the whole of antiquity; it reflects, better than any page of Polybius, the wonder of the common man at the ascendancy of Roman power from Spain to Asia Minor (ch. 8). It was originally written in Hebrew, and therefore not for the perusal of the Gentiles. But what Gentile would read it even in the Greek translation of I Mac- cabees?

In terms of political and economic organization the Jews were certainly more Hellenized after the Maccabean revolu- tion than before it. But each of the leading Jewish sects of Palestine developed a style of life which in its way kept Hel- lenization on the surface. A new devotion to the Law (whether written or oral), an increasingly scrupulous regula- tion of religious duties, a more intense meditation on the relations between Divine Wisdom and human frailty, and finally an intermittent, but very real, expectation of the turmoils of the Messianic Age reduced the impact of foreign customs. Hellenism no longer represented a mortal danger.

It is remarkable that the Palestinian Jews transmitted the new strength of their faith to those Jews who had not taken part in the Maccabean revolution and who might well have reacted unfavourably to it. This aspect of Jewish intellectual life has never been treated with the attention it deserves. As I said before, the unity of Judaism had been in question since the time of Alexander. It was defended by careful missionary work, by books of edification and by the practice of the pilgrimages to Jerusalem. But the danger of disintegration became far greater after the proclamation of an independent Jewish state in Palestine. Yet Jerusalem managed to remain the centre of Jewish religion. It might easily have been otherwise. The Mesopotamian Jews were still united to the Palestinian Jews by a common language, though the Aramaic spoken by Palestinian Jews must have presented considerable differences from the Aramaic spoken by Mesopotamian Jews. But the Mesopotamian Jews had a firm tradition of loyalty to the Seleucids, whereas the Palestinian Jews had become part of the Syrian state only about 200 B.C. The Seleucids gladly used the Mesopotamian Jews as soldiers, and the contribution of the Babylonian Jews to the defence of their city during an enemy attack was regarded as being so famous by the author of II Maccabees that he did not think it necessary to specify the circumstances (8.20). The Mesopotamian Jews did not take part in the Maccabean rebellion and apparently were unaffected by it. A few decades later they became even more remote when they passed with the whole of Mesopotamia under the control of the Parthians. Sources are strangely silent on the first hundred years of the Mesopotamian Jews under Parthian rule. Only Pliny the Elder interrupts the silence by telling us that a Zachalias Babyloniensis – surely a Jew called Zacharias – wrote a book dedicated to Mithridates (Eupator?) on the influence of precious stones on human destiny: this must have been written in Greek (*N.H.* 37.60.169). One episode is, however, enough to show that the Babylonian Jews had not drifted away. About 30 B.C. a poor young man from Babylon made an impression on the great rabbis of Jerusalem. Shemayah and Abtalion told each other (according to the Talmudic account) 'This man deserves that the Sabbath be profaned on his behalf' (*b. Yoma* 35 b). He was Hillel who – as the Talmud says elsewhere – like Ezra came from Babylon and re-established the Torah.

The Jews of Egypt represented a much more formidable problem. They spoke a different language, had a Bible of their own and thought differently. About 160 B.C. an original thinker had emerged among them, Aristobulus, who applied allegorical interpretation to the Bible and paved the way for Philo. It is difficult to understand why Clemens Alexandrinus called him a Peripatetic (*Strom.* 1.72.4), but perhaps the important point is that he was assigned to a philosophic school at all, because this was quite unusual for a Jew of the second century b.c. Aristobulus quoted Greek writers – authentic or forged – to support the truth of the Bible and the dependence of the Greeks on Jewish wisdom. He argued in particular that Plato could have known the Torah because there was an older translation than that patronized by Ptolemy Philadelphus. Aristobulus was, however, also the first to give authority to the tradition that the LXX translation was due to the initiative of Ptolemy Philadelphus and his adviser Demetrius Phalereus. He almost certainly wrote his book, which was dedicated to Ptolemy Philometor, before the publication of the Letter of Aristeas and may indeed have inspired it.

The Letter of Aristeas with its determined proclamation of the sacred value of the LXX is of course another striking indication of the degree of independence which the Egyptian Jews reached in their religious life. I do not think for a moment that the Letter of Aristeas should be taken as a Festal Scroll, something like the Book of Esther, to be read in the Alexandrian synagogues every year on the day on which (as we know from Philo) the Alexandrian Jews commemorated the translation (*De vita Mosis* 2.41). To pass over other objections, the Letter is far too long for such a purpose. But the Letter became the official account of the translation. As both Aristobulus and pseudo-Aristeas show, the Alexandrian Jews were altogether devoted to their Ptolemaic kings and displayed something like Egyptian patriotism. We know that another Jewish Egyptian historian of the second century b.c., Artapanus, made Moses the originator of the Egyptian cult of animals (Eus. *Praep. Evang.* 9.27.4): a statement which caused such pain to very respectable scholars of the nineteenth century, like J. Freudenthal (*Alexander Polyhistor*, 143–74) and A. von Gutschmid (*Kl. Schriften* ii, 184) as to persuade them that it could come only from a Jew trying to pass for a Gentile.

Another very characteristic document of this self-centred Egyptian Judaism is probably to be found in the story of *Joseph and Aseneth*. This story, the original of which is in Greek, enjoyed immense popularity among Christians from late antiquity to the late Middle Ages in a series of vernacular translations which include Ethiopian, Armenian, Old Slavonic and Middle English. Modern classical scholars forgot it. But in the last twenty years it has become fashionable again, at least in esoteric circles. Classical scholars have suddenly suspected that *Joseph and Aseneth* may be the oldest Greek novel in existence. New Testament scholars have found it relevant to the question of the nature of the Last Supper. And more generally the seekers of symbols have found a new text to interpret on their own level. The character of the book and the question of the date are indeed inseparable. But first I ought to make it clear that I share the majority opinion according to which the Greek text is of Jewish, not Christian, authorship. When the minority opinion includes the names of Erik Peterson and Arthur Darby Nock one has of course to proceed warily. But neither of them has really argued the case for a Christian novel without a Jewish model, to repeat the formulation of Nock (*Essays* ii, 900 n. 14; cf. E. Peterson, *Enciclopedia Cattolica*, s.v. Aseneth). The simple fact remains that the book tells the story of the conversion of an Egyptian girl to Judaism, and all its theology and imagery are unmistakably Jewish-Hellenistic. The Book of Genesis in the ordinary Bible leaves us curious about the mysterious Aseneth, daughter of Pothiphera, priest of On (Heliopolis), who was given as a wife by Pharaoh to Joseph and bore him the two sons Manasseh and Ephraim (41.45; 41.50–2). How beautiful was Aseneth? and why did Joseph marry a Gentile? This was an excellent point of departure for a Jew who wanted to reassert the old ties of the Jews with Egypt and at the same time make proselytes among his neighbours. Aseneth is presented as an

extremely beautiful convert to Judaism in the most romantic
circumstances. The son of Pharaoh tries to rape her with
the help of Dan and Gad, but of course the plot (in which
Jews and Egyptians are equally to blame) is discovered. The
son of Pharaoh is killed almost accidentally, and Joseph
receives the crown from Pharaoh.

As Professor G. D. Kilpatrick showed in a pioneer paper,
Judaism is presented as a mystery religion (*Expository Times*,
vol. 64 (October 1952), 4–8). Aseneth is initiated into
Judaism by partaking of a miraculous honeycomb – evidently
the biblical manna. The proselyte is not required to under-
go baptism by immersion – a rite which is presumed in the
Mishnah and which created differences on matters of detail
between the schools of Shammai and Hillel, that is, in the
first century A.D. (G. F. Moore, *Judaism* III, 109). There is
no allusion to foreign rule or to Christianity. The whole
atmosphere is that of the second or first century B.C., when
the Jews felt well rooted and powerful in the land of Egypt.
The language, which is akin to the LXX, confirms this impression.

There were all the necessary conditions for the strong
idiosyncrasies of Egyptian Judaism to develop into religious
separatism. Indeed some sort of attempt was made in this
direction, because the High Priest Onias or his son, after
escaping from Jerusalem to Egypt, founded a temple in
Leontopolis which was meant to rival Jerusalem. The schism
on the whole was a failure. Paradoxically, its Palestinian
origin may have limited its attraction for Egyptian Jews. The
temple survived until the Romans closed it in A.D. 73, but
caused little trouble. In any case the Palestinian Jews skilfully maintained and reinforced their links with Egypt,
sent their books to Egypt, and ensured acceptance of the new
festivals established in Judaea. The relatively tolerant attitude
they had adopted towards their own religious differences
in Judea may have helped them in Egypt too. Book 3 of
the Sibylline Books is a difficult text to analyse because it
was put together at the end of the first century B.C., if not

later, from material belonging to the previous 150 years. But I would consider it very probable that some sections were written by an Alexandrian Jew in support of the Maccabean rebellion, about 160–150 B.C.

We saw an example of the methods of the Palestinian Jews in the two letters which form the preface to II Maccabees. II Maccabees itself may have been meant for Egyptian Jews, and the translation of I Maccabees into Greek must have served the same purpose. We also saw that other texts were translated into Greek and diffused in Egypt from Palestine. The Book of Ben Sira was translated into Greek by his grandson after 132 B.C., and the Book of Esther was translated with additions by Lysimachus, son of Ptolemy of Jerusalem, in the fourth year of the reign of Ptolemy and Cleopatra, that is, probably in 78/77 B.C.

The Letter of Aristeas itself confirms the prestige of the Palestinian Jews in Egypt because it presents the translation of the LXX as being performed by Palestinian Jews and includes an idealized picture of the city of Jerusalem and its Temple. The newly discovered Temple Scroll is likely to throw new light on this aspect of Aristeas. We must of course await the publication of the Scroll by Professor Yigael Yadin before embarking upon comments. But what he himself has told us in preliminary communications shows that the Scroll presents a blue-print for a perfect Temple and a perfect Jewish administration coming from God, who speaks in the first person (*C.R. Acad. Inscript.* (1967), 607–19). The text, which is said to belong to the second or first century B.C., is therefore a Hebrew counterpart to the Hellenistic description of the ideal Jerusalem in Aristeas. In the present state of our knowledge it is equally possible to consider the Temple Scroll as a reaction to a Hellenized model for Jewish life, such as the Letter of Aristeas, or to regard the Letter of Aristeas as a Hellenistic equivalent to a Hebrew sectarian text like the Temple Scroll.

By avoiding the fragmentation of Judaism, and especially the secession of the Egyptian Jews, the Palestinian Jews kept the door open for exchanges with the surrounding Greek culture. The new experience of the Palestinian Jews in defending their own heritage against the attempt at whole-sale Hellenization had a favourable influence on what the Jews wrote in Greek. Much of the Jewish-Hellenistic writing of the first century B.C. and of the first century A.D. has a greater dignity and depth than the apologetics of the preceding century. Shallow historical forgeries were no longer the most important literary production. The Bible (as we can first observe in Aristobulus) was treated more seriously. Nor can we separate for this purpose what remained Jewish from what became Christian, such as St Paul's letters. It is indeed characteristic that for some of the best works, such as the Wisdom of Solomon, the Psalms of Solomon and the Assumption of Moses, there is a problem as to whether the original text was in Hebrew or in Greek.

VI

In one point, however – and it will be my final point – what remained Hellenistic in post-Maccabean Jewish culture proved disastrous. Like all the other members of the Hellenistic community the Jews learnt too little and too late about the Romans. To judge from the eulogy of Rome in I Maccabees they were outrageously misinformed even about the most obvious details of the Roman constitution. I Maccabees seems to believe that the Romans were governed by one annual magistrate, that the Senate met every day and that there was no faction in Rome. The Scroll of the War of the Sons of Light certainly shows some knowledge of the Roman army and its tactics, but even with the help of the exemplary commentary by Professor Yadin (Oxford, 1962) it is difficult to say whether the author of the Scroll understood Roman warfare. In any case the Scroll must belong to the first century A.D.

Jewish ignorance of Latin was certainly more than reciprocated by Roman ignorance of Hebrew. But the Romans of

the first century B.C. devoted great attention to the Jews. As
we have seen in the case of the Celts, and shall see in the
case of the Iranians, they were helped by Hellenistic scholars.
The authoritative exposition of Judaism for the Roman reader
of Pompey's time must have been the excursus on the Jews by
Posidonius. Posidonius reported the anti-Jewish stories circulating in Seleucid circles and apparently had a poor opinion
of contemporary Jews. But, to judge by what must derive
from him in Diodorus and Strabo, he had a sound respect
for Moses, his legislation and his followers. There is no
reason for attributing part of the section of Strabo on the
Jews to a Jewish source, as A. D. Nock hesitatingly suggested
(*Essays* II, 860–6). Posidonius seems to have transmitted his
respect for Jewish non-iconic monotheism to Varro (August.
De civ. dei 4.31), who is explicit on this matter. On the other
hand, Rome had been listening to some of the violent attacks
against the Jews which are typified in the book *Against the
Jews* by Apollonius Molon, apparently a pioneer in this
genre (Jos. *c. Apion.* 2.79; 145–8; Eus. *Praep. Ev.* 9.19).
Molon was an ambassador to Rome and passed on to his
pupil Cicero his sentiments and some of his arguments. The
position of other first-century pagan writers regarding the
Jews cannot be established with equal clarity. This is the case
with Teucer of Cyzicus who wrote six books of Jewish
history and other books on Mithridates Eupator (274 T 1
Jacoby). One would like to know whether he was a pro-
Roman or anti-Roman writer.

But no doubt subsists in regard to the most erudite of
these pagan writers on Judaism: the Milesian Alexander
Polyhistor. He was a slave, perhaps a prisoner of war, who
obtained his freedom from Sulla and worked for a long
time in Rome to produce monumental compilations on the
nations of the Near East – not to mention other erudite
works. It seems clear that he was encouraged by his Roman
patrons to put together information about the new countries
opened up to Roman conquest and influence by Sulla and
his successors. His compilation about the Jews included

extensive excerpts from Jewish and Samaritan sources in Greek and appears to have been admirably objective within its own terms of reference. Christian writers appreciated it. We cannot say whether it was read by the Romans who finished off the kingdom of Syria and turned Judaea into a Roman dependency. But Pompey knew how to take advantage of Jewish factions, customs and taboos. He had been informed.

Cicero spoke of the Jews as a 'natio nata servituti'. He was actually repeating a judgement of Apollonius Molon (Joseph. *c. Apionem* 2.148) which had been shown to be false by the Jewish defence of their Temple against Pompey. But the success of the cultural policy of Rome lent plausibility to Cicero's lie.

6

Iranians and Greeks

I

'Such things should be said beside the fire in winter-time when a man reclines full-fed on a soft couch, drinking the sweet wine and munching chick-peas – such things as: "Who and whence are you? and how old are you, good man? how old were you when the Mede came?"' (Xenophanes, fr. 18 Diehl = 22 Edmonds). The arrival of the Mede in Ionia – that is, Harpagus the Mede's conquest on behalf of Cyrus the Persian about 545 B.C. – was the beginning of a new age for Xenophanes of Colophon. He himself had left his native city as a young man in consequence of that event. At the age of 92 he was still alive, about 472 B.C. The Persian conquest of the kingdom of Lydia involved in one form or another all the Greeks of Asia Minor. The Greeks had crossed swords with the Assyrians and had had their troubles with the Egyptians, but had never lived inside a great empire – at least not after the Hittite Empire of which they remembered nothing. The Lydian rule had been easy to accept, as Lydia was soon dominated by Greek culture – open to Greek traders, artists, soldiers and oracles. Cyrus was as epoch-making for the Greeks as he was for the Jews – though the reasons were different.

The comparative philologists want us to push back the contacts between Iranians and Greeks to earlier times. E. Benveniste has argued that the words Māda and Pārsa could not have become in Greek Mēdos and Pērsēs after the end of the tenth century B.C., when the transition from the original

Greek ā to Ionic ē, and the shortening of the original long ē before a group of consonants, stopped operating (*La Persia e il mondo greco-romano*, Atti del Convegno Acc. Lincei 1965 (1966), 479–85). We would be transported into an even earlier period of Iranian-Greek relations by the word for the rose – *rhodon* – dear to Homer and presumably to his poetic masters, as he treats the ῥοδοδάκτυλος Ἡώς as a venerable formula. The rose is said to be a gift from Iran in the Bronze Age.

The poor historian, who knows nothing of relations between Greece and Iran before the sixth century, can only report. He has already some difficulty in understanding why *medism* should indicate sympathy for the Persians in the fifth century, when the Medes had been subjects of the Persians for at least sixty years. We may remind ourselves of Strabo's remark (15.3.23, p. 735): 'The Persians of all the barbarians became the most famous among the Greeks, because none of the other barbarians who ruled Asia ruled Greeks; neither were these people acquainted with the Greeks, nor yet the Greeks with the barbarians, except for a short time by distant hearsay. Homer at any rate knows neither of the empire of the Syrians nor of that of the Medes; for otherwise, since he names Egyptian Thebes and mentions the wealth there and the wealth of Phoenicia, he would not have passed by in silence that of Babylon, of Ninus and Ecbatana' (trans. H. L. Jones, Loeb).

The succession of events between the Persian conquest of Lydia about 546 and the Ionian rebellion against Persia of 500 B.C. must have filled the mind of any Greek of Asia Minor – and perhaps of any other Greek. Within a few years a previously almost unknown nation occupied Babylonia, was involved in an unsuccessful war against a fabulous queen of the distant East (which ended in the death of Cyrus), and occupied Egypt. Cambyses became famous for his impiety, the Magi rebelled – and strange stories were told about their leader. Finally Darius, who emerged victorious against the Magi, put his army in danger in another extravagant enterprise against the Scythians in southern Russia – and somehow re-emerged with his reputation hardly impaired.

Greeks were soon involved at practically every level in the process of expansion of the Persian state. According to a story in a Hellenistic historian, Agathocles of Cyzicus, Cyrus the Great gave several cities of Asia Minor to his friend Pytharchus of Cyzicus – a precedent for the gift made by Artaxerxes to Themistocles (472 F 6 Jacoby). The Athenian Miltiades, as the ruler of the Thracian Chersonesus, found himself a vassal of the Great King and one of the commanders of the Greek contingents in the Scythian expedition: the tyrants set up by the Persians in the Ionian cities were of course in the same position. The fall of the tyranny of Polycrates – with the subsequent Persian rule in Samos – was the end of one of the most brilliant centres of Greek intellectual life in the sixth century and clearly indicated that the Aegean sea had become a zone of Persian influence. A Greek or half-Greek sea captain who wrote in Greek, Scylax of Caryanda, was entrusted with the exploration of the Indus river and of the sea route from the mouth of the Indus to Suez. Greek architects, sculptors and stone cutters worked to build Pasargadae, Susa and Persepolis. Though the details are uncertain, and there is an element of subjectivity in the evaluation of the contribution of the Greeks to these works, their participation is certain (G. Gullini, *La Parola del Passato* 142–4 (1972), 13–39). Giovanni Pugliese Carratelli has recently published an inscription of the end of the sixth century from one of the quarries which served the buildings of Persepolis. The inscription says: Πυθάρχο εἰμί, 'I belong to Pytharchus' (*East and West* 16 (1966), 31–2). Pytharchus must have been a Greek contractor. As Pugliese Carratelli prudently remarks, it may be a simple coincidence that the name Pytharchus is identical with that of the man of Cyzicus who was a friend of Cyrus. This Pytharchus seems to have soon been in trouble with his subjects: he or his family may have moved into the building business at Persepolis. Greeks also helped to transport building materials to Susa under Darius, though I would not follow S. Mazzarino in his adventurous theory that the Ionians, and more precisely the Milesians, were in regular charge of the navigation from Babylonia to Susa (*La Persia e il mondo greco-romano*, 75–83). The Greeks probably brought back the word *paradeisos*, to indicate the hunting garden or enclosure, from these early contacts with Iranian architecture and landscape (the word appears first in Xenophon, among the extant sources).

Nothing is preserved of the royal chronicles composed by the Persians. Private historiography of the Greek type does not seem to have existed in Persia – or at least it left no direct or indirect trace. Perhaps the three elements of Persian education – to ride a horse, to shoot straight and to tell the truth – were not favourable to the formation of a historian. What we call the tradition on Persia is to a very great extent the tradition of subjects or enemies of Persia. But there are serious limitations even to our knowledge of the Greek reactions to Persia. Almost nothing is preserved for the period before the Ionian rebellion. Indeed the texts transmitted to us reflect a completely different situation: a situation in which the Persians are militarily inferior to the Greeks and have already been defeated at Marathon and Salamis. What was written before 500 B.C. by Scylax and perhaps by Hecataeus of Miletus has disappeared. Nor do we know what Phrynichus said in his tragedy on the capture of Miletus which was performed before the battle of Marathon and therefore in a moment of profound depression for the Greeks.

But there remains of course the possibility that Persian religious thought influenced the beginnings of Greek philosophy in this very period between 550 and 500 B.C. when nobody in Greece questioned or seemed to question the new ruling power. Those who have maintained that Pherecydes of Syros, Anaximander, Heraclitus and even Empedocles derived some of their doctrines from Persia have not always been aware that the political situation was favourable to such contacts. But this cannot be said of Professor M. L. West, the latest supporter of the Iranian origins of Greek philosophy. He certainly knows that if there was a time in which the Magi could export their theories to a Greek world ready to listen, it was the second half of the sixth century B.C. It is undeniably tempting to explain certain features of early Greek philosophy by Iranian influences. The sudden elevation of Time to a primeval god in Pherecydes, the identification of Fire with Justice in Heraclitus, Anaximander's astronomy placing the stars nearer to the Earth than the moon – these and other ideas immediately call to mind theories which we have been taught to consider Zoroastrian – or at any rate Persian – or at least Oriental.

We know even less about Achaemenid Zoroastrianism, however, than we know about Pre-Socratic thought. We must force the evidence at some point if we want to assert the dependence of the Pre-Socratics on the Magi or even generically on Oriental thought. Thanks to Dr I. Gersevitch we are now certain that Zurvān existed as a god of Time by the end of the sixth century B.C. (*Studia classica et orientalia A. Pagliaro oblata* ii (1969), 197; *Trans. Philol. Soc.* (1969) 165–200). But I have yet to meet an exact Oriental parallel to the opening sentence of the book of Pherecydes: 'Zas and Chronos have always existed, and so has Chthonie, and Chthonie got the name of Ge when Zas gave her Earth as a present' (Diels–Kranz[6], 7 fr. 1).

There is one simple consideration which makes me hesitate in this game of searching for the Zoroastrian origins of Greek thought. If we do not know much about the Pre-Socratics we know at least that their ancient readers found each of them very different from the others. If they had all been inspired by the Magi, there would be less variety of problems and solutions. As far as we can see, there is no common religious inspiration behind the earliest Greek philosophers. Where the suggestion of influence is more forceful – as in the case of Pherecydes of Syros – the contamination of the mythological and of the cosmogonic approach is more evident. This is Aristotle's judgement: 'since the "mixed" theologians, those who do not say everything in mythical form, such as Pherecydes and certain of the others, and also the Magi, name the first generator the *best* thing' (*Metaph.* 14.1091 b 8). Of course, it may be significant that Pherecydes' father had the barbarian name of Babys, but anything can be significant where nothing is certain – even the forged letter from Darius to Heraclitus inviting him to the Persian court. There was a time, not long ago, in which what Aelian *Var. Hist.* 12.32 says about Pythagoras wearing trousers was taken as evidence for his Iranian connections (W. Burkert, *Weisheit und Wissenschaft* (1962), 135; 178 n. 18).

I shall conclude this section with a cautionary tale. In 1923 Albrecht Götze published his famous paper 'Persische Weisheit in griechischem Gewande' (*Zeitschrift für Indologie und Iranistik* 2, 60 ff.). There at last one piece of definite evidence was produced for an Iranian doctrine coming to Greece. In the Hippocratic treatise *De hebdomadibus*, published for the first time in 1853 by Littré in a very corrupt Latin version, there is a theory on the correspondence between the parts of the human body and the parts of the whole world. Götze showed that this theory was also to be found in the *Greater Bundahishn*, a Zoroastrian cosmological work of the ninth century A.D., which is supposed to go back to lost sections of the *Avesta*. Götze treated the Hippocratic work as 'an erratic block in Hellas' which had come from Iran. R. Reitzenstein naturally took this as a confirmation of his theories on the Iranian origins of Greek cosmology (*Studien zum antiken Synkretismus* (1926), 119 ff.); and almost everyone was happy. Thirty years later Professor J. Duchesne-Guillemin showed the weaknesses of the whole paper by Götze in *Harvard Theological Review* 49 (1956), 115 ff. and, fashions having changed, almost everyone was happy again. In 1962 one of the greatest living Iranists, R. N. Frye, simply declared in the same Review that, with the disappearance of the evidence of the *De heb-domadibus*, nothing was left of the theory of the Iranian influences on Greek thought before Alexander (55, 261–8). When in 1965 the Accademia dei Lincei organized the successful symposium on *La Persia e il mondo greco-romano*, the *Zeitgeist* was no longer moving in the same direction. Duchesne-Guillemin recanted his refutation of Götze, as we may read in the published contributions to the symposium. He now thought that the coincidence could not be casual and that a Greek doctor operating in Persia had brought back a Persian theory in the fifth or fourth century B.C. But in 1971 M. L. West, in his very thorough analysis of the cosmology of *De hebdomadibus* (*Classical Quarterly* 65, 365–88), was again sceptical about a direct Oriental influence on it. As he says: 'The basic idea of a parallelism between the world and the human form...may well have come to Greece from the East in the sixth century. After that, however, independent development seems sufficient to account for the phenomena' (p. 387).

II

After the victory over the Persians there was much reflection on the causes of the military superiority of the Greeks. The prevailing line of explanation ascribed it to the Greek love of liberty, and this in turn raised the problem whether Greek self-reliance, courage, independence of action, etc., were due to climatic or to institutional or to racial factors. Greek poets, historians and philosophers thought about these problems, and their conclusions (as formulated in Aeschylus' *Persae*, in Herodotus, and in the Hippocratic *Airs, Waters and Places*) are a primary document of the emerging new Greek science of ethnography. Simpler explanations were obviously circulating and have left their traces in our sources – for instance, Themistocles' trick with the gullible Persian king which Aeschylus must have considered authentic enough to deserve mention (355 ff.). I should not be surprised if Ctesias' famous chronological error of putting the battle of Plataea before the battle of Salamis (*Persic.* 25) was not another popular version aimed at simplifying the story of the war: a battle on Boeotian territory between Thermopylae and Salamis would take much of the glamour out of the naval achievements of the Athenians. Ctesias, being entirely indifferent to Greek liberty and perhaps pro-Spartan, would have no difficulty in accepting such a version. But not even the reflections of Aeschylus and Herodotus were exclusively centred on the opposition between the freedom-loving Greeks and the slavery-prone Persians. After all, as Aeschylus said, Asia and Europe were sisters. There is every good reason for taking the sisters of *Persae* ll. 185–6 as Persia and Greece, which would be supported by the two young women Asia and Hellas of the Darius vase (late fourth century: C. Anti, *Archeol. Class.* 4 (1952), 24–45). In Aeschylus Darius thinks in universal terms and attributes the defeat, not to the superiority of the Greeks, but to the transgression of the divine law. He preaches the doctrine of *hybris*, which to us may seem very Greek; but to Aeschylus and Herodotus it was objectively true and therefore accessible to any wise man, Greek or not. However extravagant the Persians are made to look in Aeschylus, they are not thorough barbarians like the Egyptians of the *Suppliants*. Even more emphatically than Aeschylus, Herodotus respects the Persians and considers them capable of thinking like Greeks. When he registers the outrageous behaviour of Xerxes towards the dead body of Leonidas he emphasizes that it was an exception: 'the Persians are of all men known to me the most wont to honour valiant warriors' (7.238). He believes that the Lydians and the Greeks brought upon themselves the wrath of the Persians by their provocative conduct. He is notoriously out of sympathy with the Ionian rebellion. The victory of the Greeks, and above all the courage of the Athenians, forced him to recognize a deep difference between Persians and Greeks. It was an advantage to care for *isegoria*, equality in freedom of speech, and to feel

like a free man, not like a slave: 'and it is proved not by one
but by many instances that *isegoria* is a good thing' (5.78).
But his thinking is basically committed to the mutual understanding of Greeks and Persians. The wise among the Persians comment ironically, to Herodotus' evident delight,
that the Greeks were foolish to make war in order to revenge
the rape of a woman – and this was the Trojan war (1.4).
Herodotus very pointedly declares the Persians capable of
discussing the relative merits of democracy, oligarchy and
monarchy like any well-trained Greek sophist (3.80–2):
'When Mardonius arrived at Ionia in his voyage by the coast
of Asia he did a thing which I have set down for the wonder
of those Greeks who will not believe Otanes to have declared
his opinion among the Seven that democracy was best for
the Persians' (6.43). Modern scholars have been no less surprised than the audiences at Herodotus' lectures that he
could attribute such Hellenic ideas to the Persians. But even
a scholar with as fine an ear as K. Reinhardt was hardly able
to distinguish between authentic Persian tales and tales
attributed to the Persians by Greeks ('Herodots Perser-
geschichten' in *Vermächtnis der Antike*, 2nd ed. (1966),
133–74). Gross criteria of discrimination are sometimes
more useful than refined literary analysis. A. Demandt
recently observed that Persian monuments represent the
king with his ears uncovered, whereas in Greek iconography the Persian king is shown with his ears covered.
Thus the Herodotean story of how Phaidymia unmasked
Pseudo-Smerdis by finding out, not without personal risk,
that he had mutilated ears makes sense only within the
Greek iconographical tradition (*Iranica Antiqua* 9 (1972),
94–101): a disturbing remark for those who, like myself,
had taken this piece of Herodotus as a typical Oriental story.
However, Herodotus himself would not have been disturbed
by Professor Demandt's iconographical expertise. He liked
a certain amount of confusion. He reported that the Ionians
saved the Persian Empire by refusing to make common cause
with the Scythians at the end of Darius' expedition: he adds

that the Scythians defined the Ionians 'as the faithfullest of
slaves and the most fondly attached to their lords' (4.142).
The last chapter of Herodotus' work recalls the choice of
Cyrus the Great: 'to dwell in a poor land and exercise lord-
ship rather than to cultivate plains and be the slaves of
others' (9.122). The reader is meant to remember that
Demaratus had explained to Xerxes how Greece, having
poverty as a companion, had obtained virtue and wisdom
and consequently avoided being despotically ruled (7.102).
Memorable as the victory of the Greeks had been, the Persian Empire not only continued to exist, but to retain moral
strength for which Herodotus felt he had to account.

III

In the period between 411 and 336 B.C. Persia put far
greater pressure on Greece than she had done in the time
of Athenian naval supremacy. Persia had regained control of
the Greeks of Asia Minor and supported whatever city or
party in metropolitan Greece seemed suitable. Philip II of
Macedonia visibly imitated the Persian administrative and
military machine in his effort to transform the patriarchal
monarchy he had inherited into a large state which extended from Thrace to Thessaly and controlled much of Greece.
Thrace under a Macedonian *strategos* looked like a satrapy.
Eumenes of Cardia, though a good Greek, organized the
Macedonian chancery along the lines of the Persian one.
Arrian states explicitly that Philip created a corps of pages
on the Persian model: like their Oriental counterparts the
pages had to help the king to his horse τὸν περσικὸν τρόπον
(*Anab.* 4.13.1). Whatever their distant origins, the companions of the kings, the *hetairoi* in the strict sense, became
similar to the friends of the king in Persia.

There is, however, little evidence that in the fourth century the Persian imperial system was submitted to a searching analysis by any Greek. Our big question mark is
Ctesias, who wrote not only general books on Persia and

India, but a geographical work, a *periplous*, and a specific treatise on the tributes of Asia. The last two works are lost, and the books on Persia and India have reached us only in a Byzantine summary. The indirect tradition, however, is considerable: Diodorus and Plutarch, for instance, owe much to Ctesias. We must admit a large margin of doubt, yet what we have is disappointing. The *Persica* were filled with court intrigues and were not reliable about even these. There is no evidence that Ctesias tried to understand the Persians of his time, as Herodotus had done. Ctesias seems to be inferior to Herodotus in much the same way that his contemporary Timotheus is inferior to Aeschylus as the author of a dramatic work on the Persians. Notice that Timotheus' *Persae* shows signs of political ambition and a desire to please Sparta: Ctesias is called *philolakon* by Plutarch (*Artax.* 13.4).

Xenophon, who quotes Ctesias with respect (*Anab.* 1.8. 26–7), is not much interested in the Persian society of his time, though he had ample opportunity of observing it when he campaigned with Cyrus the Younger. Xenophon can of course tell us that a Cretan bowman had a shorter range than a Persian (*Anab.* 3.3.7) and is sufficiently acquainted with the style of the geographers to note the details of a village through which he had passed: 'fine houses, abundant supplies, and the inhabitants had wine in such quantities that they kept it in cemented cisterns' (4.2.23). The portrait of the Younger Cyrus inevitably contains some authentic details of Persian court life (1.9). But there is already in this portrait of Cyrus the idealizing tendency, the blurring of the specific Persian features which characterize the later *Cyropaedia*. As is well known, Xenophon in fact transferred many minor figures of the *Anabasis* to the *Cyropaedia*. It is irrelevant for us, though not unimportant in itself, whether certain details of the *Cyropaedia* can be interpreted as Persian legends. Arthur Christensen made out a case for the story, obviously false, of Cyrus the Great dying in his own bed surrounded by his family as a legendary Persian motif:

there are parallels in Firdausi (*Les gestes des rois dans les traditions de l'Iran antique* (1936), 126). Like his fellow-Socratic Antisthenes, Xenophon did not intend to write the history of Cyrus, but to present the picture of an ideal king. To make the point clear even to the most inattentive reader, Xenophon added a chapter to his *Cyropaedia* in which he explained how and why the Persians of his own time were different from the contemporaries of Cyrus the Great: corruption had taken the place of austerity and virility. The authenticity, which has often been questioned, of this final chapter seems to be guaranteed by several stylistic features and historical allusions. Furthermore, the same technique of opposing the reality of the present to the idealization of the past is used by Xenophon in his booklet on the constitution of Sparta. This, however, is not calculated to give a more balanced characterization of Persian life as it could be observed in the fourth century. To have more coverings on one's horse than on one's bed may be a sign of effeminacy but will not explain the rebellions of the satraps.

I find it very difficult to understand why the severe but appreciative attitude towards the Persian Empire prevailing in the fifth century yielded in the fourth century to a mixture of idealization of dead Persian kings and of gossip about contemporary court intrigues. Lack of interest in the realities of Persian political and social organization remained conspicuous in the historians who narrated its end. To judge from Arrian, the most serious books written on Alexander's campaign did not try either to evaluate the Persian state or to analyse the causes of its collapse. The less serious contemporary historians, such as Onesicritus and Clitarchus, variously combined the gossip of Ctesias with the idealization of Xenophon's *Cyropaedia* and produced sensational accounts which not even the ancient readers could quite stomach. Alluding to Onesicritus' post as steersman of Alexander's ship on the voyage down the Indus, Strabo writes that he might better be called the 'chief steersman of fantasy' (15.1.28). Like Ctesias, Onesicritus preferred to revel un-

checked in the marvels of India. 'Clitarchi probatur in-
genium, fides infamatur', says Quintilian (10.1.75). Not one
of Clitarchus' fragments, nor any of the sections of Diodorus'
Book 17 which can reasonably be traced back to him, alludes
to Persian institutions, though we know that he described
Babylon and made Alexander meet the queen of the
Amazons (fr. 10; 15–16 Jacoby).

Other historians had brief accounts of, or allusions to,
especially curious institutions: for instance, Polyclitus of
Larissa described the variety of the Great King's revenues
(128 F 3 Jacoby) and Chares of Mytilene the Great King's
voluptuous habits (125 F 2). They meant to amuse.

This situation is less surprising if we consider that Plato
and Aristotle left the political system of the Persians out of
their books on Politics. True enough, Plato's *Laws*, Book
3.693d, has the very promising statement by the Athenian:
'There are two matrices, as we may call them, of constitutions from which all others may truly be said to be derived,
the proper name of the one is monarchy, of the other democracy. The first is seen in its perfection among the Persians,
the second among my own countrymen. These are the
strands...of which all other constitutions, generally speaking, are woven' (transl. A. E. Taylor). What follows is, however, an implicit repudiation of Xenophon's idealized image
of Persian education, as Athenaeus (11.505a) perceived.
Plato denied that to be brought up in a harem by women
and eunuchs could be a good thing, and cited as confirmation the corruption in Persia of his own day. Like Isocrates
and other observers he had, of course, noticed the increasing
dependence of the Great King on foreign mercenaries. But
the Persian state as a whole is not examined. Aristotle in his
Politics is even more hasty in dismissing Persian despotism.
He alludes to the kings of Persia as tyrants who must take
precautions for their own safety (1284 b 1; 1313 a 38); and
he sees the Persians, like the Scythians, the Thracians and
Celts, as an expanding nation which holds military strength
in honour (1324 b 11). He also notices in a typical aside that

the Persian kings do not play an instrument, but have music played to them (1339 a 34). The Persian Empire was no part of the political world. To what extent Persia figured in his *Nomima Barbarika*, his account of the institutions of the barbarians, it is impossible to say. The few surviving fragments speak about Carians, Etruscans and the Greek ancestors of the Romans.

We should have to form a very different picture of Aristotle if the Arabic text of a letter from him to Alexander were substantially authentic. This letter, which was known from quotations by mediaeval Arabic and Jewish writers, was published in a shorter version in 1891 by J. Lippert and in a longer version in 1970 by Jozef Bielawski with a commentary by Marian Plezia. Independently of Plezia, the longer version was studied by Samuel Stern in his little book *Aristotle on the World State* (1968). Stern intended to publish a critical edition and commentary of the longer text in collaboration with Oswyn Murray, but his premature death intervened. His study, which inclines to accept the authenticity of the letter, is more critical and subtle than the book by Bielawski and Plezia, both resolute supporters of its authenticity. The two features of the letter which concern us are, first, the advice to Alexander to deport to Europe, if not all the Persians, at least their aristocracy, and secondly, the prefiguration of a universal state in which 'all enjoy safety and quiet, dividing their day into parts, part for the welfare of the body, part for education and attention to that noble pursuit, philosophy' (transl. S. M. Stern, pp. 7–8). Aristotle would patronize the idea of a universal state in Messianic terms, but pursue at the same time the traditional line of Greek revenge against the Persians by asking for their deportation.

The Aristotle we had previously known only once and very guardedly admitted the possibility of the political unification of the world. He did so in the famous paragraph of *Politics* 7 (1327 b 29): 'the Greek race participates in both characters, just as it occupies the middle position geographically, for it is both spirited and intelligent: hence it continues to be free and to have very good political institutions and to be capable of ruling all mankind, if it attains constitutional unity'. There is a considerable difference between this cool, hypothetical and isolated statement and the enthusiastic support for a world state of the Persian type as suggested by the new text. Even if we take *Politics* 7 as an early product of Aristotle and date the letter to Alexander after 330 B.C., we should have to admit a change of mind of which the other works preserve no evidence. The new letter inevitably reminds us of the inscriptions and of Philo exalting the benefits of the Augustan peace. Is this an illusion?

The combination of Greek nationalism and cosmopolitanism which is characteristic of the letter would of course be compatible with a date in the Roman imperial period. To quote an example on the nationalistic side, Hippocrates is made to give a fiercely patriotic answer to King Artaxerxes in an exchange of letters. Hippocrates, rather forgetting his own Hippocratic oath, tells the king: 'I cannot heal the barbarians who are enemies of the Greeks' (Hercher, *Epistolographi Graeci*, ed. Didot, p. 290). This is a part of a short epistolary novel, which must belong to the Roman age because one of the individuals involved in the correspondence is called Paetus. I should therefore not be surprised to find a forger of the imperial age attributing to Aristotle in the same breath the patriotic idea of deporting the Persians and the premonition of a universal state.

IV

Trivialities of this kind must have a place in our story because they are indicative of the mood in which for centuries after Alexander the Greeks went on thinking about the Persians. Pride in the old victories against them persisted in narrow nationalistic terms. On the other hand, the new versions of the idea of a universal state propounded by Alexander and later by the Romans inevitably recalled Persia as an antecedent. But if the Persians of old lingered on in the imagination of Hellenistic man, the contemporary Persians were almost forgotten. Polybius quotes words which Demetrius of Phalerum wrote at the beginning of the third century B.C.: who would have believed fifty years ago that 'the name of the Persians would have perished utterly – the Persians who were masters of almost the whole world?' (29.21.4). Polybius' contemporary Agatharchides of Cnidus wrote ten books about Asia which must have contained a long section on Achaemenid Persia. One can prove almost mathematically that he could not have dealt at any length with the Iran of his own time, the Iran of the increasingly prosperous and strong Parthian state. We know of course of the Seleucids' strenuous efforts to maintain their hold over the Iranian plateau which alone made it possible for them to compete with Egypt and Macedonia. It was probably in the reign of Antiochus IV, in the middle of the second century B.C., that Ecbatana was transformed into a *polis* called *Epiphaneia* (Steph. Byz., s.v. Agbatana). Thirty or forty years later the Arsacids of Parthia put an end to Seleucid rule in all parts of Iran and consolidated their frontier along the Euphrates. During the two centuries of struggle for the control of the various populations and societies of Iran the Seleucids must have tried to collect information about them. If so, almost nothing of this information survives. Modern scholars have to learn from stray remarks in literary sources or from epigraphical discoveries that in the first century B.C. Antiochus of Commagene was proud of reckoning the great Darius as his ancestor, or that there was in Persia a king or prince called Artaxerxes, who lived long enough to be registered among the *Macrobii* by Lucian or Pseudo-Lucian, 15. We may of course be misled by our evidence, but what we have indicates a profound indifference of the Hellenistic – even of the Seleucid – intellectuals to the re-emergence of a new Iran from the ruins of the Achaemenid one.

This lack of interest was not reciprocal. As we know, the Parthians did their best to keep in touch with the Greek world. Some of their kings called themselves philhellene and were clean-shaven in the Greek fashion. The Seleucid era survived, and the Arsacid era which competed with it was an imitation. The Parthian coins were inscribed in Greek. The Parthian scribes abandoned Aramaic for Greek as the international language, and Greek individuals rose high in the administration of the state. The royal letter to Seleucia on the Eulaeus (Susa) and the Greek poems of the same place have become exhibit pieces of correct Greek (*Suppl. Epigr. Graecum* VII, 1–33). King Artavasdes of Armenia wrote tragedies and histories in Greek, and the pitiful story of the end of Crassus is for ever linked with the performance of Euripides' *Bacchae* at Artaxata (Plut. *Crassus* 33). No doubt there was another side of the picture which the slow and complicated transformation of the Parthian dialect into a written language helps to conceal. Iranian legends were elaborated and transmitted to posterity; the adventures of Hercules were absorbed into an Iranian context and inspired some of the feats of the hero Rostam. Professor Minorski and his pupil Professor M. Boyce have given us new guidance on this (quoted in A. Pagliaro–A. Bausani, *La letteratura persiana* (1968), 60; 70).

But we must confine ourselves to the Greek side. The Greek subjects of the Arsacids took an active part in the intellectual life of the country in which they lived, explored the land and wrote down its history. What apparently their ancestors had not done under the Seleucids, they did under the Parthians. Their anxiety to get the best instruction in Greek and the reluctance of good teachers to come to them is exemplified by a story in Plutarch which, though famous, bears repetition. The rhetorician Amphicrates of Athens went as a visiting lecturer to Seleucia on the Tigris, but when he was offered a permanent chair he replied that a stew-pan would not contain a dolphin (*Lucullus* 22.5).

Apollodorus of Artemita is the best known of the Greek writers from Parthia. He was one of Strabo's major sources for his native land and must have lived in the first decades of the first century B.C. F. Altheim wants him to be the main source of the Parthian books of Trogus Pompeius as well (*Weltgeschichte Asiens* I (1947), 2–24), but all we can say is that Trogus must ultimately have availed himself of information transmitted by a Parthian Greek of the Sullan age (W. W. Tarn, *The Greeks in Bactria and India*, 2nd ed. (1951), 45–9). Pliny the Elder had among his geographical sources Isidore of Charax, whose pamphlet on the *Parthian Stations* still survives: he too was a Greco-Parthian. Finally, the same Pliny mentions a Dionysius of Charax who prepared a memorandum for the adoptive son of Augustus, Gaius, on the occasion of the Oriental mission of the year I B.C. (*N.H.* 6.141).

The evidence shows an intensive study of Parthian history and geography by Greeks who lived in Parthia and also indicates that the Romans exploited it to get to know the Parthians. The disaster of Carrhae had taught them a lesson. It is not by chance that what we have about the Parthians is mainly in Strabo and Trogus, two writers of the Augustan age when Rome had to decide whether to live with the Parthians. The Romans needed the advice of Greek ethnographers to deal with the Parthians, just as they needed their knowledge to establish themselves in Gallia and Spain. The only difference is that there were no Greek ethnographers resident in Gaul or Spain: they had to be fetched from other Greek centres. For Parthia the Romans had no need to import Greeks. The parallelism is reinforced when we notice that Posidonius was as conspicuous a student of Parthian affairs as he was of Celtic life. Several of his books of history were devoted to the relations between Parthia and the Seleucids, and the brilliancy with which he presented Parthian life and manners matched the style of his Celtic sketches. Here again it is Athenaeus who recognized that Posidonius' pages contained material for an anthology. One can only regret that he confined his anthology to Parthian banqueting habits. There were certainly more important things in Posidonius, but the scene of the formal meal at the

Parthian court is good enough: 'The man who enjoys the title of king's friend has no share at his table but sits on the ground while the king reclines above him on a high couch. He eats dog-fashion what the king throws to him' (4.152f–153a; 87 F 5 Jacoby).

The Romans studied the Parthians seriously, and used Greek historians and geographers to provide them with the necessary information. This incidentally explains why the only reliable piece of information about the religious situation in Iran during the Hellenistic period is to be found in Strabo Book 15. What the learned men of Alexandria and Athens wrote for Greek consumption about the Magi was, as we shall soon see, wishful thinking. There is a curious appendix to this story. Flavius Josephus, who was evidently aware of the Roman interest in the Parthians, repeatedly promised to provide further details about them and the last Seleucids in his *Jewish Antiquities*. He apparently never made good his promises; about ten times he says 'as we have shown elsewhere', but the 'elsewhere' turns out to be no-where. The simplest solution is to assume that he intended to write a history of the late Seleucids and of the Parthians, but did not live long enough to do so. A history of Parthia was written not much later by Arrian, the historian of Alexander the Great.

V

The Hellenistic Greeks living outside Parthia never seem to have taken a serious intellectual interest in what was happening in Parthia; they became interested in a disembodied Persian thought, without any relation to political or social realities. What circulated in the Hellenistic world under the names of Zoroaster and of the Magi was a mixture of some genuine information with much arbitrary imagination. Groups of Iranians living in Asia Minor have been considered responsible for at least some of the doctrines which passed under the name of the Magi. This is not impossible. Strabo (15.3.15, p. 733), Dio Chrysostomus (36.39) and

Pausanias (5.27.5) all more or less explicitly claimed to
have met Magi of the West. The Persians, like the Jews,
may have enjoyed writing what they expected their Greek
neighbours to be anxious to hear. But the origins and
development of the western legend of Persian wisdom have
little to do with this Persian diaspora in the West. The origins
go back to the second half of the fifth century B.C. when
Xanthus the Lydian spoke of Zoroaster and dated him six
thousand years earlier. Xanthus also referred to the Magi
without apparently connecting them with Zoroaster
(*F.Gr.H.* 765 F 31–2 Jacoby). As Xanthus also spoke of
Empedocles (fr. 33), and Empedocles left an unfinished
poem on the Persian wars (Diog. Laert. 8.57), it has been
suspected with more phantasy than necessity that Empedocles, too, spoke of Zoroaster. Herodotus of course knew of
the Magi as a Median tribe, but does not mention Zoroaster;
and Magus was a term current in fifth-century Greek to
indicate a quack. In Ctesias Zoroaster became a king of
Bactria surrounded by Magi, and Trogus Pompeius still
repeated this story at the end of the first century B.C. (Justin
1.1.9). Allusions to Zoroaster must have become a commonplace with fourth-century historians. Theopompus knew
that Ormuzd and Ahriman would each have to govern the
world for three thousand years before the start of the
golden age in which men will lose their shadows (115 F 65
Jacoby). Dinon, the historian of Persia, connected Zoroaster
etymologically with the stars (690 F 5 Jacoby). But it was
Plato who made Persian wisdom thoroughly fashionable,
though the exact place of Plato in the story is ambiguous and
paradoxical. Plato seems never to have mentioned Zoroaster.
The appearance of Zoroaster in the *Alcibiades Maior* (122a)
is only one of the many arguments which make this dialogue
almost certainly spurious. It is also very doubtful whether
Plato meant the myth of Er to be taken as a genuine Oriental
myth; but the reputation of Plato's connections with
Chaldaea and Magi spread. The *Academicorum Index Herculanensis*, which belongs to the first century B.C. at the latest,

has a Chaldaean at Plato's deathbed (ed. Mekler, p. 13), whereas Seneca knows that some Magi found themselves in Athens when Plato died (*ep.* 58.31). The ironical Epicurean Colotes, who lived two generations later than Plato, mocked at his alleged borrowings from Zoroaster (Proclus, *In Rempubl.* 2.109 Kroll), which indicates that the connection was a well-established opinion about 280–250 B.C. By then the Academy had become increasingly interested in Oriental wisdom. It was therefore natural to ask whether Er was Zoroaster – a question which was widely debated in antiquity, as we know from Proclus. Among the direct pupils of Plato, Philippus of Opus, if he is the author of the *Epinomis*, and Hermodorus wrote about astrological theology and mysticism; Heraclides Ponticus gave the title *Zoroaster* to a work – perhaps a dialogue – meant to express his disagreement with Plato on points of natural philosophy (Plut. *Adv. Colot.* 14.1115A); Eudemus knew about the importance of Time in the doctrines of the Magi (Bidez–Cumont, *Les Mages Hellénisés* II, 69 n. 15). Aristotle never wrote the book on the Magi which was attributed to him: it was probably the work of the second-century Peripatetic Antisthenes. But he seems to have put Zoroaster six thousand years before Plato's death (Plin. *N.H.* 30.3), a dating which is also attributed to Eudoxus, though Eudoxus died before Plato: another example of how untrustworthy information on these matters can be. We have, however, no particular reason to doubt that Aristotle considered the Magi more ancient, and therefore presumably more respectable, than the Egyptian priests. His pupil and friend Aristoxenus, who came originally from Pythagorean circles, knew that Pythagoras had been a pupil of the Chaldaean Zaratas: another version of the name Zarathustra (fr. 13 Wehrli). This is the earliest evidence known to me for the total confusion between Chaldaean priests and Magi (F. Jacoby's doubts, *F.Gr.H.* 273 F 94, seem to me unjustified). By the first century B.C., when the pseudo-Platonic *Axiochus* was probably written, it was usual to attribute to a Magus the right kind of information about the Other World. A little later Philo in his least Jewish treatise, *Quod omnis probus liber sit* (11.74), can refer to the Persian doctrines on the virtues of God as something everyone must know about.

I have held back as long as I could the name of Eudoxus because there is so little one can honestly say about the man who has been credited with a central role in introducing an unpolitical and half-fanciful Persian culture to the Greeks. Eudoxus lived for sixteen months in Egypt, apparently with a recommendation from King Agesilaus of Sparta to King Nectanebus; but he never visited Persia. His acquaintance with Zoroastrian thought seems to have been limited to generalities on the conflict between good and evil. Cicero treated him as a great authority on astrology, but what exactly he knew is a mystery. Works on prognostics circulated under his name, and Sextus Empiricus knew one of them (*Adv. Mathem.* 5.1). A calendar with meteorological information was ascribed to him. We have still far to go before we can convince ourselves that Eudoxus is the great Orientalizer depicted by Werner Jaeger and after him by Cumont and Bidez.

What seems to have happened is that the name of Zoroaster, like that of Hermes Trismegistus, became the centre of attraction for any sort of speculation which had something to do with astrology, the after-life and more generally the mysteries of nature. I could not indicate a dividing line between what was thought to be Egyptian and what was thought to be Chaldaean, even in the muddled form in which Chaldaean and Zoroastrian became synonymous. But new-fangled speculations gained prestige from the academic and Peripatetic admiration for the wisdom of Zoroaster and, no doubt, mixed Platonic ideas with those alleged to be Oriental. Pliny says that Hermippus, a Peripatetic scholar who lived about 200 B.C., 'commented upon two millions of verses left by Zoroaster, besides completing indexes to his several works' (*N.H.* 30.4). We know Hermippus as a biographer. He does not have the reputation of being the most scrupulous scholar of his time; but he wrote a book on the Magi and had a definite theory about the Oriental origins of Greek wisdom; he thought, for instance, that Pythagoras had appropriated the doctrines of Jews and Thracians (Joseph. *c. Apion.* 1.165). The information about the two million lines – that is, 800 volumes – must come from Hermippus himself. Take it as you may, it must mean that at least a few works were circulating in Alexandria which purported to be Zoroastrian. Not much help can come from the story in the *Dīnkart* (Bidez–Cumont, *Mages Hellénisés* II, 137) that 'the evil-destined villain Alexander' had the Avesta translated into the Greek language. Nor should I put much faith in the passage of Syncellus (271 D, p. 516 Bonn) that Ptolemy Philadelphus had Latin, Egyptian, and Chaldaean books translated for his library. I know of only one serious claim that the *Gathas* were read in the Hellenistic-Roman world. This was made by David Flusser for Yasna 44.3–5 in comparison with a Christian passage in *Sibylline Oracles* VIII, ll. 439–55 (*Numen*, Suppl. XXI (1972), 171–5). Though the similarity indicated by Flusser is real, it only proves that religious imagery travels. But some of the books later circulating under the name of Zoroaster or of some Magi may already have been fabricated before Hermippus' time. Four books on Nature by Zoroaster dedicated to King Cyrus were known to Proclus (*In Rempubl.* 2.109 Kroll). A different edition of this text had been available to Clemens Alexandrinus (*Strom.* 5.14.103.2). Five books on *Astrologumena* by Zoroaster are mentioned by the *Suda*. None of these books can be certainly dated before 200 B.C. The four books on Nature are in any case a work written by somebody who knew Plato's *Republic*. Forgeries made in the name of Zoroaster and of other Magi must have been frequent. We are fortunate in knowing from Porphyry that Plotinus gave him the task of demonstrating the forgery of an Apocalypse attributed to Zoroaster (*Vita Plot.* 16): his success in finding the real date of the Book of Daniel must have been the origin of the new assignment. We may be certain that Porphyry performed his part with devastating results. It is clear from Pliny (*N.H.* 30.8) that he knew of a book under the name of the Magus Osthanes, and later books circulated under this name. The Christian writers Justin and Lactantius quote a prophecy under the name of the Magus Hystaspes. The fact that Roman authorities prohibited its circulation is sufficient to prove that it belonged to the anti-Roman prophecies characteristic of the second and first centuries B.C. (Bidez–Cumont, *Mages Hellénisés* I, 215–17).

We can almost visualize the birth of one of these forgeries in the composition of the *Borysthenicus* by Dio Chrysostomus at the end of the first century A.D. His Magian hymn may imitate some Persian or rather pseudo-Persian text, and is somehow supported by the later Mithraic bas-relief of Dieburg, but, as we have it, it is Dio's own creation (A. D. Nock, *Essays on Religion and the Ancient World* II, 607). These forgeries depended on the theory that Greek thinkers had learnt some basic truths from Oriental sages; a theory which was applied to Egypt by Hecataeus of Abdera about 300 B.C. (Diodor. 1.96–8) and extended to the whole of the East by Sotion, the writer of biographies of Greek philosophers whom we know as one of the main sources of Diogenes Laertius. By the time of Sotion (200 B.C.) Democritus had become another thorough student of Persian wisdom; indeed it was said that Xerxes himself had given him Magi and Chaldaeans as teachers (Diog. Laert. 9.34). On the other hand, these forgeries proved the theory from which they derived their existence. In a sense it is not very important whether they were meant to be Egyptian or Persian. Though forgeries of Hermes Trismegistus indicated interest in Egypt (or perhaps the national pride of Hellenized Egyptians) and forgeries of Zoroaster indicated interest in Persia (or perhaps the national pride of Hellenized Persians), readers were likely to absorb pseudo-Hermes together with pseudo-Zoroaster, and indeed, pseudo-Abraham, without national preferences. What mattered was the total impression of the dependence of Greek culture on barbarian wisdom. There was furthermore the additional implication that such barbarian wisdom was better absorbed at its sources (the pseudo-texts) than in its Greek derivatives: Zoroaster and Hermes Trismegistus must have been superior to Plato and Pythagoras if they were their masters.

The time was approaching in which the Pythagorean or Platonic Numenius of Apamaea could ask his question: 'What is Plato but an Atticizing Moses?' (fr. 10, p. 130 Leemans). Such a question underlined the most obvious historical consequence of the subordination of Greek thought to Oriental wisdom, that is, the change from the conquest of truth through reason to the acquisition of truth through revelation. But it is not this consequence, however momentous, which concerns me here. It is rather the process leading to this conclusion which I should like to make clear. We started with Greek intellectuals facing Persia as a state with its own political organization, its moral code and, vaguely in the background, its religion. Slowly, for good or bad reasons, the interest in the political organization decreased – while the Persian moral code was idealized beyond the limits of credibility. The next step, which is later than Alexander, was to concentrate attention on the wisdom of the Magi and of their spiritual leader, Zoroaster. Zoroaster became a great master without hindrance because nobody really cared to know what he had been or what he had written or truly inspired. This Zoroaster and these Magi were to a great extent the work of the imagination of the Greeks themselves or of Hellenized foreigners (perhaps connected with the Iranian communities of the West). They have a claim to special attention because of their curious connection with the thinkers of the Platonic and Aristotelian schools. But, taken in themselves, the Zoroastrian forgeries go to join all the other forgeries which consoled and distracted the individual in the Hellenistic period by giving him notions of purity, of the after-life, of dependence on the stars, and of magic techniques: the Zoroastrian forgeries were only one category among many in the process of strong revulsion from the political interests of classical Greece. Behind the forgeries there was of course the living and powerful reality of genuine Zoroastrianism, but the forgeries were only its pale shadow.

I am not sure that one can calculate the consequences of being fed on forgeries. But I am sure that it makes a difference if a civilization, like the Hellenistic civilization, not only loses faith in its own principles, but admires its own forgeries as manifestations of a foreign civilization. This would never have happened if the Greeks had taken more care to learn foreign languages. If they had read Babylonian, Persian and Egyptian texts in the original their reactions would have been at a different level. The Romans never had the problem of comparing Pythagoras and Plato with Hermes Trismegistus or Zoroaster because they had neither Pythagoras nor Plato. But they never forgot that Persia and indeed Egypt were real countries which posed political problems. Furthermore, when they had to turn to foreign civilizations they chose that of the Greeks, the language of which was accessible. Finally – and this is curious, too – they made only one acquisition in the Persian market of ideas: this was Mithras. What Mithraism was before its Romanization is a question into which I have no intention of entering. But Roman Mithraism, with its system of collegia, hierarchy of initiates, the probable absence of professional priests, the emphasis on struggle and victory, and its unintellectual crudity, was exactly the opposite of the refined deception Hellenistic Greeks practised upon themselves by cultivating Zoroastrianism. It was a real cult and reinforced the loyalty of soldiers, functionaries and traders to the Roman state. In Roman Egypt there is plenty of evidence for the new cult of Mithras, but in Ptolemaic Egypt, as far as I know, the only evidence for an authentically practising Mazdean is the third-century B.C. epigram by Dioscorides, in which a Persian slave begs his master 'not to defile fire' on his body and not to pour water on his corpse (*Anth. Pal.*

7.162). If Mithras, according to Lucian, did not speak Greek (*Deorum Concil.* 9), he certainly spoke Latin.

* * *

Once again we have come up against the dilemma of Hellenistic civilization. It had all the instruments for knowing other civilizations – except command of languages. It had all the marks of a conquering and ruling upper class – except faith in its own wisdom. Many of the politically-minded Greeks chose Rome; many of the religiously-minded went to an imaginary Persia and an imaginary Egypt. With the decline of the political fortunes of Hellenism the self-doubting questions increased and encouraged the weak-minded and the unscrupulous to offer easy ways out in texts which could not be genuine.

The Romans took advantage of Greek technical co-operation to build up their knowledge of barbarian lands and ultimately to conquer the Greeks themselves. But they had put themselves, intellectually speaking, in a very strong position by learning Greek and turning their knowledge of Greek to the creation of a common Italian culture in the Latin language. The Greeks explored the world of the Celts, the Jews, the Persians and of the Romans themselves. The Romans conquered Celts, Jews and the Greeks themselves. After having been defeated by the Persians or Parthians, they took care, with the help of Greek historians and geographers, to avoid another disaster, and they succeeded at least for three centuries. We take our story only up to the time of Augustus; and therefore we are not supposed to know what happened, to Greeks as well as Romans, when a new barbarian sect decided to preach in Greek to the Gentiles. Let me conclude by applying to Hellenistic civilization the words about Protestantism to be found in a lecture by Arthur Darby Nock, the great Cambridge scholar from whom I have learnt most about my present subject. Hellenism, I would say in Nock's words, 'had to stand before the world absolutely on its own merits, as a frank and deliberate compromise between tradition, or, if you prefer it, revelation and reason; and when you make such a compromise you cannot cry, "Stop" ' (*Essays on Religion and the Ancient World* I, 339).

Select Bibliography

GENERAL AND CHAPTER I :

The Greeks and their neighbours in the Hellenistic world

Leo, F., *Geschichte der römischen Literatur* I, Berlin 1913

Täubler, E., *Imperium Romanum* I, Leipzig 1913

Trüdinger, K., *Studien zur Geschichte der griechisch-römischen Ethno-graphie*, Basel 1918

Bayet, J., 'Les origines de l'arcadisme romain', *Mél. Écol. Rome* 38 (1920), 60–143

Gsell, S., *Histoire ancienne de l'Afrique du Nord* IV, Paris 1920

Norden, E., *Die germanische Urgeschichte in Tacitus Germania*, Leipzig 1920

Holleaux, M., *Rome, la Grèce et les monarchies hellénistiques au IIIe siècle av. J.C.*, Paris 1921

Cichorius, C., *Römische Studien*, Berlin 1922

Schnabel, P., *Berossos und die babylonisch-hellenistische Literatur*, Leipzig 1923

Kroll, W., 'Römer und Griechen', in *Studien zum Verständnis der römischen Literatur*, Stuttgart 1924

Uxkull-Gyllenband, W., *Griechische Kultur-Entstehungslehren*, Berlin 1924

Meyer, E., *Blüte und Niedergang des Hellenismus in Asien*, Berlin 1925

Schnayder, G., *Quibus conviciis alienigenae Romanos carpserint*, Cracoviae 1928

Altheim, F., *Griechische Götter im alten Rom*, Giessen 1930

Hoffmann, W., *Rom und die griechische Welt im 4. Jahrhundert* (*Philologus*, Supplbd. 27, 1), Leipzig 1934

Schubart, W., 'Die religiöse Haltung des frühen Hellenismus', in *Der Alte Orient* 35, 2 (1937)

Fuchs, H., *Der geistige Widerstand gegen Rom in der antiken Welt*, Berlin 1938

Bickerman, E. J., 'Sur une inscription grecque de Sidon', *Mélanges Syriens offerts à M. R. Dussaud* I (Paris 1939), 91–9

Norden, E., *Aus altrömischen Priesterbüchern*, Lund 1939

151

Select bibliography

Carcopino, J., 'Les origines pythagoriciennes de l'Hercule romain', *Aspects mystiques de la Rome païenne* (Paris 1942), 173–206

Vogt, J. (ed.), *Rom und Karthago*, Leipzig 1943

Krattinger, L., *Der Begriff des Vaterlandes im republikanischen Rom*, diss. Zürich 1944

Ninck, M., *Die Entdeckung von Europa durch die Griechen*, Basel 1945

Altheim, F., *Weltgeschichte Asiens im griechischen Zeitalter* I–II, Halle 1947–8

Mazzarino, S., *Introduzione alle guerre puniche*, Catania 1947

Gagé, J., *Apollon romain*, Paris 1955

Lévêque, P., 'Lycophronica', *Rev. Ét. Anc.* 57 (1955), 36–56

Hanell, K., 'Zur Problematik der älteren römischen Geschichtsschreibung', *Histoire et historiens dans l'Antiquité*, Fondation Hardt Entretiens IV (Vandoeuvres–Genève 1956), 147–70

Picard, G.-Ch., *Le monde de Carthage*, Paris 1956

Bayet, J., *Histoire politique et psychologique de la religion romaine*, Paris 1957

Dunbabin, T. J., *The Greeks and their Eastern Neighbours*, London 1957

Bowra, C. M., 'Melinno's Hymn to Rome', *Journ. Roman Studies* 47 (1957), 21–8

Stier, H. E., *Roms Aufstieg zur Weltmacht und die griechische Welt*, Köln 1957

Badian, E., *Foreign Clientelae*, Oxford 1958

Drexler, H., 'Iustum Bellum', *Rh. Museum* 102 (1959), 97–140

Hadas, M., *Hellenistic Culture*, New York 1959

Momigliano, A., 'Atene nel III secolo a.C. e la scoperta di Roma nelle storie di Timeo di Tauromenio', *Rivista Storica Italiana* 71 (1959), 529–56 = *Terzo Contributo* (Roma 1966), 23–53

Heinze, R., *Vom Geist des Römertums*, 3rd ed., Darmstadt 1960

Latte, K., *Römische Religionsgeschichte*, München 1960

Momigliano, A., 'Linee per una valutazione di Fabio Pittore', *Rend. Acc. Lincei* 15 (1960), 310–20 = *Terzo Contributo* (Roma 1966), 55–68

Fraenkel, E., *Elementi Plautini in Plauto*, Firenze 1960

Grecs et Barbares, Fondation Hardt Entretiens VIII, Vandoeuvres-Genève 1961

Eddy, S. K., *The King is Dead: Studies in the Near Eastern Resistance to Hellenism 334–31 B.C.*, Lincoln, Nebraska 1961

Klingner, F., *Römische Geisteswelt*, 4th ed., München 1961

Nilsson, M. P., *Geschichte der griechischen Religion* II, 2nd ed., München 1961

Oppermann, H. (ed.), *Römertum*, Darmstadt 1962

Knoche, U., *Vom Selbstverständnis der Römer*, Heidelberg 1962

Gabba, E., 'Il latino come dialetto greco', *Miscellanea di Studi Alessandrini in memoria di A. Rostagni* (Torino 1963), 188–94

Hellegouarc'h, J., *Le vocabulaire latin des relations et des partis politiques sous la République*, Paris 1963

Musti, D., 'Sull'idea di συγγένεια in iscrizioni greche', *Ann. Scuola Normale Pisa* 2, 32 (1963), 225–39

Select bibliography

Waszink, J. H., 'Some Observations on the Appreciation of the "Philosophy of the Barbarians" in Early Christian Literature', *Mélanges Christine Mohrmann* (Utrecht 1963), 41–56

Calderone, S., *Pistis–Fides*, Messina 1964

Fraenkel, E., 'Zur Geschichte des Wortes Fides', *Rh. Museum* 71 (1916), 187–99=*Kleine Beiträge zur klassischen Philologie* i (Roma 1964), 15–26

Fraenkel, E., *Kleine Beiträge zur klassischen Philologie* ii, Roma 1964

Seel, O., *Römertum und Latinität*, Stuttgart 1964

Le rayonnement des civilisations grecque et romaine sur les cultures périphériques (8e Congrès International d'Archéologie Classique, Paris 1963), Paris 1965

Gabba, E., 'Considerazioni sulla tradizione letteraria sulle origini della Repubblica' in *Les origines de la République romaine*, Fondation Hardt Entretiens xiii (Vandoeuvres-Genève 1966), 135–69

Mazzarino, S., *Il pensiero storico classico* i–iii, Bari 1966

Klein, R. (ed.), *Das Staatsdenken der Römer*, Darmstadt 1966

Weische, A., *Studien zur politischen Sprache der römischen Republik*, Münster 1966

Wieacker, F., 'Die XII Tafeln in ihrem Jahrhundert', *Les origines de la République romaine*, Fondation Hardt Entretiens xiii (Vandoeuvres-Genève 1966), 293–356

Will, E., *Histoire politique du monde hellénistique* i–ii, Nancy 1966–7

Walbank, F. W., *A Historical Commentary on Polybius* i–ii, Oxford 1957–67

Haffter, H., *Römische Politik und römische Politiker*, Heidelberg 1967

Oppermann, H. (ed.), *Römische Wertbegriffe*, Darmstadt 1967

Schefold, K., *Die Griechen und ihre Nachbarn*, Berlin 1967

Josifovic, S., 'Lykophron', in Pauly–Wissowa, *R.E.*, Suppl. 11 (1968), 888–930

Schneider, C., *Kulturgeschichte des Hellenismus* i–ii, München 1967–69

Heurgon, J., *Rome et la Méditerranée Occidentale jusqu'aux guerres puniques*, Paris 1969

Salmon, E. T., *Roman Colonization under the Republic*, London 1969

Peters, F. E., *The Harvest of Hellenism*, New York 1970

Schlumberger, D., *L'Orient hellénisé*, Paris 1970

Ampolo, C., 'Analogie e rapporti fra Atene e Roma arcaica', *Parola del Passato* 141 (1971), 443–57

Deininger, J., *Der politische Widerstand gegen Rom in Griechenland 217–86 v. Chr.*, Berlin 1971

Torelli, M., 'Il santuario di Hera a Gravisca', *Parola del Passato* 136 (1971), 44–67

Boyancé, P., *Études sur la religion romaine* (Roma 1972), 91–152 (on *fides*)

Klose, P., *Die völkerrechtliche Ordnung der hellenistischen Staatenwelt in der Zeit von 280 bis 168 v. Chr.*, München 1972

Nock, A. D., *Essays on Religion and the Ancient World*, Oxford 1972

Timpe, D., 'Fabius Pictor und die Anfänge der römischen Historiographie', *Aufstieg und Niedergang der römischen Welt* (ed. H. Temporini) ii (Berlin 1972), 928–69.

Select bibliography

Garbarino, G., *Roma e la filosofia greca dalle origini alla fine del II secolo a.C.* I–II, Torino 1973

Sherwin-White, A. N., *The Roman Citizenship*, 2nd ed., Oxford 1973

Yaron, R., 'Semitic Elements in Early Rome', *Daube Noster* (ed. A. Watson) (Edinburgh and London 1974), 343–57

Hahn, I., 'Die Hellenisierung Karthagos und die punisch-griechischen Beziehungen im 4. Jahrhundert v.u.Z.', *Hellenische Poleis* II (1974), 841–54

Momigliano, A., *Contributo alla storia degli studi classici (e del mondo antico)* I–V in 7 vols., Roma 1955–75

Id., 'The Fault of the Greeks', *Daedalus*, Spring 1975, 9–20

CHAPTER 2:
Polybius and Posidonius

Fustel de Coulanges, N. D., *Polybe*, Amiens 1858

Norden, E., *Agnostos Theos*, Leipzig 1913

Frank, T., *Roman Imperialism*, New York 1914

Reinhardt, K., *Poseidonios*, München 1921

Mühl, M., *Poseidonios und der plutarchische Marcellus*, Berlin 1925

Reinhardt, K., 'Poseidonios über Ursprung und Entartung', *Orient und Antike* 6 (1928)

Pasquali, G., 'Cesare, Platone e Posidonio', *Studi Ital. Fil. Class.* n.s. 8 (1931), 297–310 = *Pagine Stravaganti* I (Firenze 1968), 332–43

Pohlenz, M., *Antikes Führertum*, Leipzig 1934

Edelstein, L., 'The Philosophical System of Posidonius', *Amer. Journ. Phil.* 57 (1936), 286–325

Wilamowitz-Moellendorff, U. von, 'Athenion und Aristion', *Sitz. Berl. Akad.* (1923), 7, 39–50 = *Kleine Schriften* v, 1 (Berlin 1937), 204–19

Trouard, M. A., *Cicero's Attitude towards the Greeks*, Chicago 1942

Mioni, E., *Polibio*, Padova 1949

Gigante, M., 'La crisi di Polibio', *Parola del Passato* 16 (1951), 33–53

Klotz, A., 'Die Benutzung des Polybios bei römischen Schriftstellern', *Studi Ital. Filol. Class.* 25 (1951), 243–65

Ziegler, K., 'Polybios', in Pauly–Wissowa, *R.E.* 21, 2 (1952), 1440–578

De Sanctis, G., *Storia dei Romani* IV, 2, 1, Firenze 1953

Reinhardt, K., 'Poseidonios von Apameia', in Pauly–Wissowa, *R.E.* 22, 1 (1953), 558–826

Fritz, K. von, *The Theory of the Mixed Constitution in Antiquity; a critical analysis of Polybius' political ideas*, New York 1954

De Miranda, A., 'La irreligiosidad de Polibio', *Emerita* 24 (1956), 27–65

Gabba, E., *Appiano e la storia delle guerre civili*, Firenze 1956

Schmitt, H. H., 'Hellenen, Römer und Barbaren. Eine Studie zu Polybios', *Wissenschaftl. Beilage zum Jahresbericht 1957–58 d. Hum. Gymnasiums Aschaffenburg*, 38–48

Heurgon, J., 'The Date of Vegoia's Prophecy', *Journ. Roman Studies* 49 (1959), 41–5

Select bibliography

Nock, A. D., 'Posidonius', *Journ. Roman Studies* 49 (1959), 1–15

Cole, Th., 'The Sources and Composition of Polybius VI', *Historia* 13 (1964), 440–86

Pédech, P., 'Un grec à la découverte de Rome. L'exil de Polybe', *Orpheus* 11 (1964), 123–40

Pédech, P., *La méthode historique de Polybe*, Paris 1964

Brunt, P. A., 'Reflections on British and Roman Imperialism', *Comparative Studies in Society and History* 7 (1965), 267–88

Candiloro, E., 'Politica e cultura in Atene da Pidna alla guerra mitridatica', *Studi Classici e Orientali* 14 (1965), 134–76

Dahlheim, W., *Deditio und Societas*, diss. München 1965

Pédech, P., 'Les idées religieuses de Polybe', *Rev. Hist. Rel.* 167 (1965), 35–68

Strasburger, H., 'Poseidonios on Problems of the Roman Empire', *Journ. Roman Studies* 55 (1965), 40–53

Eisen, K. F., *Polybiosinterpretationen*, Heidelberg 1966

Fraser, P., 'The Alexandrian View of Rome', *Bull. Soc. Arch. Alexandrie* 42 (1967), 1–16

Lehmann, G. A., *Untersuchungen zur historischen Glaubwürdigkeit des Polybios*, Münster 1967

Musti, D., 'Polibio e la democrazia', *Ann. Scuola Normale Pisa* 2, 36 (1967), 155–207

Badian, E., *Roman Imperialism in the Late Republic*, 2nd ed., Oxford 1968

La Penna, A., *Sallustio e la 'rivoluzione' romana*, Milano 1968

Petzold, K. E., *Studien zur Methode des Polybios*, München 1969

Badian, E., *Titus Quinctius Flamininus, Philhellenism and Real-Politik*, Cincinnati 1970

Tejera, A. Díaz, 'La constitucion politica en cuanto causa suprema en la historiografía de Polibio', *Habis* 1 (1970), 31–43

Abel, K., 'Die kulturelle Mission des Panaitios', *Antike und Abendland* 17 (1971), 119–43

Brunt, P. A., *Italian Manpower, 225 B.C.–A.D. 14*, Oxford 1971

Meister, K., *Kritik und Polemik bei Polybios*, Habilitationsschrift Saarbrücken 1971

Weinstock, S., *Divus Julius*, Oxford 1971

Badian, E., *Publicans and Sinners*, Oxford 1972

Desideri, P., 'L'interpretazione dell'impero romano in Posidonio', *Rend. Ist. Lombardo* 106 (1972), 481–93

Walbank, F. W., *Polybius*, Berkeley, Los Angeles, London 1972

Gabba, E. (ed.), *Polybe*, Fondation Hardt Entretiens xx, Vandoeuvres–Genève 1974

Bengtson, H., 'Das Imperium Romanum in griechischer Sicht', *Kleine Schriften zur Alten Geschichte* (München 1974), 549–67

Momigliano, A., *Polybius between the English and the Turks*, J. L. Myres Memorial Lecture, Oxford 1974

Gabba, E., 'Storiografia greca e imperialismo romano', *Riv. Storica Ital.* 86 (1974), 625–42

Select bibliography

CHAPTER 3:
The Celts and the Greeks

Bienkowski, P. von, *De simulacris Barbararum Gentium apud Romanos*, Cracow 1900

Bienkowski, P. von, *Die Darstellungen der Gallier in der hellenistischen Kunst*, Wien 1908

Jullian, C., *Histoire de la Gaule* I, Paris 1908

Norden, E., *Die Germanische Urgeschichte in Tacitus Germania*, Leipzig 1920

Kendrick, T. D., *The Druids: A Study in Keltic Prehistory*, London 1927

Bienkowski, P. von, *Les Celtes dans les arts mineurs Gréco-romains*, Cracow 1928

Clerc, M., *Massalia*, Marseille 1927–9

Jacobsthal, P.–Neuffer, E., 'Gallia Graeca', *Préhistoire* 2 (1933), 1–64

Broche, G.-E., *Pythéas le Massaliote*, Paris 1935

Brunel, J., 'La légende de Comanus', *Rev. Philologie* 10 (1936), 333–44

Jacobsthal, P., *Early Celtic Art*, 2 vols., Oxford 1944

Grenier, A., *Les Gaulois*, Paris 1945 (new ed. with bibl. by L. Harmand, Paris 1970)

Hubert, H., *Les Celtes depuis l'époque de La Tène et la civilisation celtique*, 2nd ed., Paris 1950

Mette, H. J., *Pytheas von Massalia*, Berlin 1952

Jannoray, J., *Ensérune*, Paris 1955

Actes du colloque sur les influences helléniques en Gaule, Dijon 1958

Powell, T. G. E., *The Celts*, London 1958

Tierney, J. J., 'The Celtic Ethnography of Posidonius', *Proceedings of the Royal Irish Academy* 60 (c) (1959–60), 189–275 (with text and translation)

Sartori, F., 'Galli Transalpini transgressi in Venetiam', *Aquileia Nostra* 31 (1960), 1–40

Villard, F., *La céramique grecque de Marseille (vi^e–ive siècle)*, Paris 1960

Eydoux, H. P., *La France Antique*, Paris 1962

Joffroy, R., *Le trésor de Vix*, Paris 1962

On the elegy about the Galatians (Page D., *Greek Literary Papyri* 1, 463): V. Bartoletti, *Studi Ital. Filol. Class.* 34 (1962), 25–30; W. Richter, *Maia* 15 (1963), 93–117; W. Peek, *ib.*, 199–218

De Vries, J., *La religion des Celtes*, Paris 1963

Jackson, K. H., *The Oldest Irish Tradition: A Window on the Iron Age*, Cambridge 1964

Benoit, F., *Recherches sur l'hellénisation du Midi de la Gaule*, Aix-en-Provence 1965

Dion, R., 'La renommée de Pythéas dans l'Antiquité', *Rev. Ét. Lat.* 43 (1965), 443–66

Piggott, S., *Ancient Europe*, Edinburgh 1965

Carpenter, Rhys, *Beyond the Pillars of Heracles* (New York 1966), 143–98

Dion, R., 'Pythéas explorateur', *Rev. Phil.* 40 (1966), 191–216

Select bibliography

Morel, J.-P., 'Les Phocéens en Occident: certitudes et hypothèses', *Parola del Passato* 108–10 (1966), 378–420

Piggott, S., *The Druids*, London 1968

Barruol, G., *Les peuples préromains du Sud-Est de la Gaule*, Paris 1969 (*Revue Archéologique Narbonnaise*, Suppl. 1)

Chadwick, N., *The Celts*, Harmondsworth 1970

Harmand, J., *Les Celtes au Second Age du Fer*, Paris 1970

Hatt, J. J., *Celts and Gallo-Romans*, trans. J. Hogarth, Geneva 1970

Lepore, E., 'Strutture della colonizzazione focea in Occidente', *Parola del Passato* 130 (1970), 19–54

Duval, P. M., *La Gaule jusqu'au milieu du Ve siècle* i–ii, Paris 1971

Hansen, E. V.: A bibliography of the Gallic statues in the art of Pergamon in E. V. Hansen, *The Attalids of Pergamon*, 2nd ed. (Ithaca and London 1971), 496–7

Mac Niocaill, G., *Ireland before the Vikings* (The Gill History of Ireland 1), Dublin and London 1972

Bar-Kochva, B., 'On the Sources and Chronology of Antiochus I's Battle against the Galatians', *Proceed. Cambridge Philol. Society* 199 (1973), 1–8

Kleiner, F. S., '*Gallia Graeca, Gallia Romana* and the Introduction of Classical Sculpture in Gaul', *Amer. Journ. Arch.* 77 (1973), 379–90

Markale, J., *Les Celtes*, Paris 1973

Clavel-Lévêque, M., 'Das griechische Marseille', *Hellenische Poleis* (ed. E. Ch. Welskopf) (Berlin 1974), vol. ii, 855–969

Clemente, G., *I romani nella Gallia meridionale*, Bologna 1974

CHAPTER 4:

The Hellenistic discovery of Judaism

Bernays, J., *Theophrastos' Schrift über Frömmigkeit*, Berlin 1866

Freudenthal, J., *Hellenistische Studien* 1–2, Breslau 1875

Willrich, H., *Juden und Griechen vor der Makkabäischen Erhebung*, Göttingen 1895

Reinach, Th., *Textes d'auteurs grecs et romains relatifs au Judaïsme*, Paris 1895

Schürer, E., *Geschichte des jüdischen Volkes im Zeitalter Jesu Christi* i–iii, 4th ed., Leipzig 1901–9 (the first volume is brought up to date in an English translation, Edinburgh 1973)

Daiches, S., *The Jews in Babylonia in the Time of Ezra and Nehemiah*, London 1910

Peters, N., *Das Buch Jesus Sirach oder Ecclesiasticus*, Münster 1913

Böhl, F. M. Th., 'Die Juden im Urteil der griechischen und römischen Schriftsteller', *Theolog. Tijdschrift* 48 (1914), 371–89; 473–98

Pfister, F., 'Eine jüdische Gründungsgeschichte Alexandrias', *Sitz. Ak. Heidelberg* (1914), no. 11

Hill, G. F., *A Catalogue of the Greek Coins of Palestine*, London 1914

Norden, E., 'Jahve und Moses in hellenistischer Theologie', *Festgabe A. v.*

Harnack (Tübingen 1921), 292–301 = *Kleine Schriften* (Berlin 1966), 276–85

Büchler, A., 'Ben Sira's Conception of Sin and Atonement', *Jew. Quart. Rev.* n.s. 13 (1922–3), 303–35; 461–502; 14 (1923–4), 53–83

Schlatter, A., *Geschichte Israels von Alexander d.Gr. bis Hadrian*, 3rd ed., Stuttgart 1925

Täubler, E., *Tyche*, Leipzig 1926

Bousset, W., *Die Religion des Judentums im späthellenistischen Zeitalter*, 3rd ed., Tübingen 1926

Lévy, I., *La légende de Pythagore de Grèce en Palestine*, Paris 1927

Heinemann, I., 'Antisemitismus' in Pauly–Wissowa, *R.E.*, Suppl. v (1931), 3–43

Lewy, H., 'Hekataios von Abdera περὶ Ἰουδαίων', *Zeitschr. Neut. Wiss.* 31 (1932), 117–32

Leipoldt, J., *Antisemitismus in der Alten Welt*, Leipzig 1933

Sellers, O., *The Citadel of Beth Zur*, Philadelphia 1933

Bertram, G., 'Der Hellenismus in der Urheimat des Evangeliums', *Archiv für Religionsw.* 32 (1935), 265–81

Rankin, O. S., *Israel's Wisdom Literature*, Edinburgh 1936

Lewy, H., 'Aethiopier und Juden in der antiken Literatur', *Monatsschrift Gesch. Wiss. Judentums* 81 (1937), 65–71

Pfeiffer, R. H., 'Hebrews and Greeks before Alexander', *Journ. Bibl. Liter.* 56 (1937), 91–101

Lewy, H., 'Aristotle and the Jewish Sage', *Harv. Theol. Rev.* 31 (1938), 205–35

Braun, M., *History and Romance in Graeco-Oriental Literature*, Oxford 1938

Jaeger, W., 'Greeks and Jews', *Journ. Religion* 18 (1938), 127–43 = *Scripta Minora* (Roma 1960), II, 169–83

Dornseiff, F., *Echtheitsfragen antik-griechischer Literatur*, Berlin 1939

Schneider, C., 'Die griechischen Grundlagen der hellenistischen Religionsgeschichte', *Arch. Religionswiss.* 36 (1939), 300–47

Heinemann, I., 'The Attitude of the Ancient World towards Judaism', *Rev. Religion* 4 (1940), 385–400

Kroll, W., 'Phokylides' in Pauly–Wissowa, *R.E.* 20, 1 (1941), 503–10

Liebermann, S., *Greek in Jewish Palestine*, New York 1942

Finkelstein, L., 'Pre-Maccabean Documents in the Passover Haggadah', *Harv. Theol. Rev.* 36 (1943), 1–38

Marcus, R., 'Antisemitism in the Hellenistic-Roman World' in K. S. Pinson (ed.), *Essays on Antisemitism*, 2nd ed. (New York 1946), 61–78

Reifenberg, A., *Ancient Jewish Coins*, 2nd ed., Jerusalem 1947

Täubler, E., 'Jerusalem 201 to 199 B.C.E. On the history of a messianic movement', *Jew. Quart. Rev.* 37 (1946–7), 1–30; 125–37; 249–63

Hölscher, G., 'Drei Erdkarten. Ein Beitrag zur Erderkenntnis des hebräischen Altertums', *Sitz. Heidelb. Akad.* (1948), 34, 3

Heichelheim, F. M., 'Ezra's Palestine and Periclean Athens', *Zeitschr. Relig. Geistesgesch.* 3 (1951), 251–3

Cardascia, G., *Les Archives des Murašû*, Paris 1951

Select bibliography

Driver, G., *Aramaic Documents of the Fifth Century B.C.*, Oxford 1954

Cadbury, H. J., 'The Grandson of Ben Sira', *Harv. Theol. Rev.* 48 (1955), 219–25

Pritchard, J. B. (ed.), *Ancient Near Eastern Texts*, 2nd ed., Princeton 1955 (Supplement 1969)

Loewe, R., 'The Earliest Biblical Allusion to Coined Money', *Palest. Expl. Quart.* 87 (1955), 141–50

Katz, P., 'The Old Testament Canon in Palestine and Alexandria', *Zeitschr. Neut. Wiss.* 47 (1956), 191–217

Tcherikover, V. A.–Fuks, A. *Corpus Papyrorum Judaicarum* I, Cambridge, Mass. 1957

Mazar, B., 'The Tobiads', *Israel Exploration Journal* 7 (1957), 137–45; 229–38

McCown, C. C., 'The 'Araq el-Emir and the Tobiads', *The Biblical Archaeologist* 20 (1957), 63–76

Lewis, D. M., 'The First Greek Jew', *Journ. Semit. Studies* 2 (1957), 264–6

Smith, M., 'The Image of God: Notes on the Hellenization of Judaism', *Bull. John Rylands Library* 40 (1957–8), 473–512

Gutman, Y., *The Beginnings of Jewish Hellenistic Literature* I–II, Jerusalem 1958–63 (in Hebrew)

Tcherikover, V., *Hellenistic Civilization and the Jews*, Philadelphia 1959

Schunck, K. D., 'Drei Seleukiden im Buche Kohelet?', *Vetus Testam.* 9 (1959), 192–201

Rudolph, W., *Vom Buch Kohelet*, Münster 1959

Dornseiff, F., *Kleine Schriften* I: *Antike und Alter Orient*, 2nd ed., Leipzig 1959

Feldman, L. H., 'The Orthodoxy of the Jews in Hellenistic Egypt', *Jewish Social Studies* 22 (1960), 215–37

Auerbach, E., 'Der Aufstieg der Priesterschaft zur Macht im alten Israel', *Vet. Test. Stud.* 9 (1962), 236–49

Kerenyi, K., *Die griechisch-orientalische Romanliteratur*, 2nd ed., Darmstadt 1962

Naveh, J., 'The Excavations at Mesad Hashavyahu', *Israel Exploration Journal* 12 (1962), 89–113

Bickerman, E. J., *From Ezra to the Last of the Maccabees*, New York 1962

Liebermann, S., *Hellenism in Jewish Palestine*, 2nd ed., New York 1962

Schaller, B., 'Hekataios von Abdera über die Juden', *Zeitschr. Neutest. Wiss.* 54 (1963), 15–31

Yoyotte, J., 'L'Égypte ancienne et les origines de l'antijudaïsme', *Rev. Hist. Rel.* 163 (1963), 133–43

Cross, F. M., 'The Discovery of the Samaria Papyri', *The Biblical Archaeologist* 26 (1963), 110–21

Speiser, E. A., *Genesis* (Anchor Bible), New York 1964

Gottwald, N. K., *All the Kingdoms of the Earth: Israelite Prophecy and International Relations in the Ancient Near East*, New York 1964

Eissfeldt, O., *Einleitung in das Alte Testament*, 3rd ed., Tübingen 1964

Zeitlin, S., *The Rise and Fall of the Judaean State* I, Philadelphia 1964

Select bibliography

Sisti, A., 'Riflessi dell'epoca premaccabaica nell'Ecclesiastico', *Riv. Bibl.* 12 (1964), 215–56

Galling, K., *Studien zur Geschichte Israels im persischen Zeitalter*, Tübingen 1964

Loretz, O., *Qohelet und der Alte Orient*, Freiburg–Basel–Wien 1964

Walter, N., 'Frühe Begegnungen zwischen jüdischem Glauben und hellenistischer Bildung in Alexandrien', in E. Ch. Welskopf (ed.), *Neue Beiträge zur Geschichte der Alten Welt* I (Berlin 1964), 367–78

Liftshitz, B., 'L'Hellénisation des Juifs de Palestine', *Rev. Bibl.* 72 (1965), 520–38

Musti, D., 'Lo Stato dei Seleucidi', *Studi Classici e Orientali* 15 (1966), 61–197

Cross, F. M., 'Aspects of Samaritan and Jewish History in Late Persian and Hellenistic Times', *Harv. Theol. Rev.* 59 (1966), 201–11

Bickerman, E. J., *Four Strange Books of the Bible*, New York 1967

Nikiprowetzky, V. 'Temple et Communauté', *Rev. Ét. Juiv.* 126 (1967), 7–25

Nikiprowetzky, V., 'Le Nouveau Temple', *ib.* 130 (1971), 1–30

Kanael, B., 'Altjüdische Münzen', *Jahrb. für Numism.* 17 (1967), 159–298

Auscher, D., 'Les relations entre la Grèce et la Palestine avant la conquête d'Alexandre', *Vetus Testamentum* 17 (1967), 8–30

Goodenough, E., *Jewish Symbols in the Greco-Roman Period*, 13 vols., New York 1953–68 (among the discussions notice E. Bickerman, *Syria* 44 (1967), 131–61)

Fischel, H. A., 'Studies in Cynicism and the Ancient Near East: the transformation of a *Chria*', *Religions in Antiquity. Essays E. R. Goodenough* (Leiden 1968), 372–411

Robert, L., *Fouilles d'Aï Khanoum* I (Paris 1973), 207–37 = *C.R. Acad. Inscr.* (1968), 416–57

Porten, B., *Archives from Elephantine*, Berkeley 1968

Ackroyd, P. R., *Exile and Restoration*, London 1968

Delling, G., *Bibliographie zur jüdisch-hellenistischen und intertestamentarischen Literatur 1900–1965*, Berlin 1969

Gager, J. G., 'Pseudo-Hecataeus Again', *Zeitschr. Neutest. Wiss.* 60 (1969), 130–9

Weinberg, S. S., 'Post-Exilic Palestine. An Archaeological Report', *Proceedings of the Israel Academy* 4 (1969–70), 78–97

Riis, P. J., *Sukas I. The North-East Sanctuary and the First Settling of Greeks in Syria and Palestine*, Copenhagen 1970

Ackroyd, P. R., *Israel under Babylon and Persia*, Oxford 1970

Preuss, H. D., *Verspottung fremder Religionen im Alten Testament*, Stuttgart 1971

Smith, M., *Palestinian Parties and Politics that Shaped the Old Testament*, New York 1971

Grelot, P., *Documents araméens d'Egypte*, Paris 1972

Brock, S. P., 'The Phenomenon of the Septuagint', *Oudtestam. Studiën* 17 (1972), 11–36

Forkman, G., *The Limits of the Religious Community*, Lund 1972

Select bibliography

Gager, J. G., *Moses in Greco-Roman Paganism*, Nashville 1972 (cf. the review by M. Stern, *Anglican Theological Review* 55 (1973), 94–8)
Hengel, M., *Judentum und Hellenismus*, 2nd ed., Tübingen 1973 (Engl. transl., London 1974)
Braun, R., *Kohelet und frühhellenistische Populärphilosophie*, Berlin 1973
Naveh, J., 'Some Semitic Epigraphical Considerations on the Antiquity of the Greek Alphabet', *Amer. Journ. Archaeol.* 77 (1973), 1–8
Hanson, P. D., 'Zechariah 9 and the Recapitulation of an Ancient Ritual Pattern', *Journ. Bibl. Lit.* 92 (1973), 37–58
Stern, M. and Murray, O., 'Hecataeus of Abdera and Theophrastus on Jews and Egyptians', *Journ. Egypt. Arch.* 59 (1973), 159–68
Smitten, W. Th. in der, 'Historische Probleme zum Kyrosedikt und zum Jerusalemer Tempelbau von 515', *Persica* 6 (1974), 167–78

CHAPTER 5:
Greeks, Jews and Romans from Antiochus III to Pompey

Geffcken, J., *Komposition und Entstehungszeit der Oracula Sibyllina*, Leipzig 1902
Charles, R. H., *The Book of Enoch*, Oxford 1912
Burkitt, F. C., *Jewish and Christian Apocalypses*, London 1914
Heinemann, I., 'Poseidonios über die Entwicklung der jüdischen Religion', *Monatsschrift Gesch. Wiss. Judentums* 63 (1919), 113–21
Meyer, E., *Ursprung und Anfänge des Christentums* I–III, Stuttgart 1921–3
Thackeray, H. St John, *The Septuagint and Jewish Worship*, London 1923
Willrich, H., *Urkundenfälschung in der hellenistisch-jüdischen Literatur*, Göttingen 1924
Kolbe, W., *Beiträge zur syr. und jüdischen Geschichte*, Stuttgart 1926
Kittel, G., *Die Probleme des palästinischen Spätjudentums und das Urchristentum*, Stuttgart 1926
Bickerman, E. J., 'Ritualmord und Eselskult', *Monatsschrift Gesch. Wiss. Judentums* 71 (1927), 171–87, 255–64
Charles, R. H., *A Critical and Exegetical Commentary on the Book of Daniel*, Oxford 1929
Moore, G. F., *Judaism in the First Centuries of the Christian Era: the age of the Tannaim* I–III, Cambridge, Mass. 1927–30
Bickerman, E. J., 'Zur Datierung des Pseudo-Aristeas', *Zeitschr. Neut. Wiss.* 29 (1930), 280–98
Momigliano, A., *Prime linee di storia della tradizione Maccabaica*, Torino 1931 (reprint with a new bibl. Amsterdam 1966)
Lagrange, M.-J., *Le Judaïsme avant Jésus Christ*, Paris 1931
Bickerman, E. J., 'Ein jüdischer Festbrief vom Jahre 124 v. Chr.', *Zeitschr. Neut. Wiss.* 32 (1933), 233–54
Volz, P., *Die Eschatologie der jüdischen Gemeinde im neutestamentlichen Zeitalter*, Tübingen 1934
Ginsburg, M. S., 'Sparta and Judaea', *Class. Philol.* 29 (1934), 117–22

Select bibliography

Bickerman, E. J., 'La Charte Séleucide de Jérusalem', *Rev. Ét. Juives* 100 (1935), 4–35

Bickerman, E. J., 'Un document relatif à la persécution d'Antiochos IV Épiphane', *Rev. Hist. Religions* 115 (1937), 188–223

Loewe, H. (ed.), *Judaism and Christianity*, II, *The Contact of Pharisaism with Other Cultures*, London 1937

Bickerman, E. J., *Der Gott der Makkabäer*, Berlin 1937

Heinemann, I., 'Wer veranlasste den Glaubenszwang der Makkabäerzeit?', *Monatsschrift Gesch. Wiss. Judentums* 82 (1938), 145–72

Bickerman, E. J., 'Sur une inscription grecque de Sidon', *Mélanges Syriens offerts à M. R. Dussaud* I (Paris 1939), 91–9

Swain, J. W., 'The Theory of the Four Monarchies', *Classical Philology* 35 (1940), 1–21

Torrey, C. C., 'The Letters Prefixed to Second Maccabees', *Journ. Am. Orient. Soc.* 60 (1940), 119–50

Peretti, A., *La Sibilla babilonese nella propaganda ellenistica*, Firenze 1943

Bickerman, E. J., 'Héliodore au temple de Jérusalem', *Ann. Inst. Phil. Hist. Orient. Slav.* 7 (1939–44), 5–40

Torrey, C. C., 'The Older Book of Esther', *Harv. Theol. Rev.* 37 (1944), 1–4

Bickerman, E. J., 'The Colophon of the Greek Book of Esther', *Journ. Bibl. Liter.* 63 (1944), 339–62

Bickerman, E. J., 'Une proclamation séleucide relative au temple de Jérusalem', *Syria* 25 (1946–8), 67–85

Abel, F.-M., 'Hellénisme et orientalisme en Palestine au déclin de la période séleucide', *Rev. Bibl.* 53 (1946), 385–402

Kahle, P., 'Die Septuaginta. Prinzipielle Erwägungen', *O. Eissfeldt Festschrift* (Halle 1947), 161–80

Seeligmann, I. L., *The Septuagint Version of Isaiah*, Leiden 1948

Abel, F.-M., *Les Livres des Maccabées*, Paris 1949

Pfeiffer, R. H., *History of New Testament Times*, New York 1949

Bickerman, E. J., 'The Date of the Testaments of the Twelve Patriarchs', *Journ. Bibl. Liter.* 69 (1950), 245–60

Spiro, A., 'Samaritans, Tobiads and Judahites in Pseudo-Philo', *Proceed. Amer. Acad. Jewish Research* 20 (1951), 279–355

Bickerman, E. J., 'Notes on the Greek Book of Esther', *Proceed. Amer. Acad. Jewish Research* 20 (1951), 101–33

Bickerman, E. J., 'Sur la chronologie de la sixième Guerre de Syrie', *Chronique d'Égypte* 27 (1952), 396–403

Bickerman, E. J., 'La chaîne de la tradition pharisienne', *Revue Biblique* 59 (1952), 44–54

Bentzen, A., *Daniel*, 2nd ed., Tübingen 1952

Bammel, E., 'Zum jüdischen Märtyrerkult', *Theolog. Literaturz.* 78 (1953), 119–26

Ackroyd, P. R., 'Criteria for the Maccabean Dating of O.T. Literature', *Vetus Testam.* 3 (1953), 113–32

Norden, E., 'Das Genesiszitat in der Schrift vom Erhabenen', *Abh. Berl. Akad.* (1954), no. 1 = *Kleine Schriften* (Berlin 1966), 286–313

Select bibliography

Stein, S., 'The Liturgy of Hanukkah and the First Two Books of Maccabees', *Journ. Jewish Studies* 5 (1954), 100–6; 148–55

Lévy, I., 'Les deux Livres des Maccabées et le Livre Hébraique des Hasmonéens', *Semitica* 5 (1955), 15–36

Farmer, W., *Maccabees, Zealots and Josephus*, New York 1956

Mowinckel, S., *He that cometh*, Oxford 1956

Tcherikover, V., 'The Ideology of the Letter of Aristeas', *Harv. Theol. Rev.* 51 (1958), 59–85

Cross, F. M., *The Ancient Library of Qumrân*, London 1958

Testuz, M., *Les idées religieuses du Livre des Jubilés*, Genève 1960

Muilenburg, J., 'The Son of Man in Daniel and the Ethiopic Apocalypse of Enoch', *Journ. Bibl. Lit.* 79 (1960), 197–209

Stern, M., 'The Death of Onias III', *Zion* 25 (1960), 1–16 (Hebrew)

Smith, M., 'The Dead Sea Sect in Relation to Ancient Judaism', *New Testament Studies* 7 (1960–1), 347–60

Kreissig, H., 'Der Makkabäeraufstand. Zur Frage seiner sozialökonomischen Zusammenhänge und Wirkungen', *Studii Classice* 4 (1962), 143–75

Yadin, Y., *The Scroll of the War of the Sons of Light against the Sons of Darkness*, Oxford 1962

Wright, G. E., 'The Samaritans at Shechem', *Harv. Theol. Rev.* 55 (1962), 357–66

Kocsis, E., 'Ost–West Gegensatz in den Jüdischen Sibyllen', *Nov. Testam.* 5 (1962), 105–10

Giblet, J., 'Eupolème et l'historiographie du Judaïsme hellénistique', *Ephem. Theol. Lovan.* 39 (1963), 539–54

Jaubert, A., *La Notion d'alliance dans le Judaïsme aux abords de l'ère chrétienne*, Paris 1963

Wacholder, B. Z., 'Pseudo-Eupolemus' Two Greek Fragments on the Life of Abraham', *Hebrew Union College Annual* 34 (1963), 83–113

Tcherikover, V., 'Was Jerusalem a "Polis"?', *Israel Explor. Journal* 14 (1964), 61–78

Walter, N., *Der Thoraausleger Aristobulos*, Berlin 1964

Russell, D. S., *The Method and Message of Jewish Apocalyptic, 200 B.C.–A.D. 200*, London 1964

Porteous, N. W., *Daniel. A Commentary*, London 1965

Burchard, Chr., *Untersuchungen zu Joseph und Aseneth*, Tübingen 1965

Lévy, I., *Recherches esséniennes et pythagoriciennes*, Genève–Paris 1965

Walter, N., 'Zu Pseudo-Eupolemos', *Klio* 43–5 (1965), 282–90

Morkholm, O., *Antiochus IV of Syria*, Copenhagen 1966

Cardauns, B., 'Juden und Spartaner', *Hermes* 95 (1967), 317–24

Murray, O., 'Aristeas and Ptolemaic Kingship', *Journ. Theol. St.* 18 (1967), 337–71

Arenhoevel, D., *Die Theokratie nach dem 1. und 2. Makkabäerbuch*, Mainz 1967

Philonenko, Marc, *Joseph et Aséneth. Introduction, texte critique, traduction et notes*, Leiden 1968

Vermès, G., *The Dead Sea Scrolls in English*, Harmondsworth 1968

Select bibliography

Baer, Y., 'The Persecution of Monotheistic Religion by Antiochus Epiphanes', *Zion* 33 (1968), 101–24 (Hebrew)

Osten-Sacken, P. von der, *Die Apokalyptik in ihrem Verhältnis zu der Prophetie und Weisheit*, München 1969

Larcher, C., *Études sur le Livre de la Sagesse*, Paris 1969

Denis, A.-M., 'Héraclès et ses cousins de Judée', *Hommages M. Delcourt* (Bruxelles 1970), 168–78

Stern, M., 'Strabo on Jews', *G. Alon Memorial Volume* (Tel Aviv 1970), 169–91 (Hebrew)

Black, M., *Apocalypsis Henochi Graece*; A.-M. Denis, *Fragmenta Pseudepigraphorum quae supersunt graeca*, Leiden 1970

Nikiprowetzky, V., *La troisième Sibylle*, Paris 1970

Lebram, J. C. H., 'Apokalyptik und Hellenismus im Buche Daniel', *Vetus Testam.* 20 (1970), 503–24

Kippenberg, H. G., *Garizim und Synagoge*, Berlin 1971

Delcor, M., *Le Livre de Daniel*, Paris 1971

Schalit, A., 'Die Denkschrift der Samaritaner an König Antiochos Epiphanes', *Annual Swedish Theological Institute* 8 (1970–1), 131–83

Neusner, J., *The Rabbinic Traditions about the Pharisees before 70* I–III, Leiden 1971

Noack, B., *Spätjudentum und Heilsgeschichte*, Stuttgart 1971

Hanson, P. D., 'Jewish Apocalyptic against its Near Eastern Environment', *Rev. Bibl.* 78 (1971), 31–58

Howard, G. E., 'The Letter of Aristeas and Diaspora Judaism', *Journ. Theol. Studies* N.S. 22 (1971), 337–48

Bunge, J. G., *Untersuchungen zum zweiten Makkabäerbuch*, Bonn 1971

Meinhold, A., 'Die Geschichte des Sinuhe und die Alttestamentliche Diasporanovelle', *Wiss. Zeitschrift Univ. Greifswald* 20 (1971), 277–81

Giovannini, A.–Müller, H., 'Die Beziehungen zwischen Rom und den Juden im 2. Jh. v. Chr.', *Museum Helveticum* 28 (1971), 156–71

Moraldi, L., *I Manoscritti di Qumran*, Torino 1971

Flusser, D., 'The Four Empires in the Fourth Sibyl and in the Book of Daniel', *Israel Oriental Studies* 2 (1972), 148–75

Places, E. des, 'Le Dieu Incertain des Juifs', *Journ. Savants* (1973), 289–94

Middendorp, T., *Die Stellung Jesu Ben Siras zwischen Judentum und Hellenismus*, Leiden 1973

Collins, John J., 'The Provenance of the Third Sibylline Oracle', *Bull. Institute Jewish Studies* 2 (1974), 1–18

Timpe, D., 'Der römische Vertrag mit den Juden von 161 v. Chr.', *Chiron* 4 (1974), 133–52

West, S., 'Joseph and Asenath', *Class. Quart.* N.S. 24 (1974), 70–81

Stern, M., *Greek and Latin Authors on Jews and Judaism* I, Jerusalem 1974

Momigliano, A., 'The Second Book of Maccabees', *Classical Philology* 70 (1975), 81–91

Select bibliography

CHAPTER 6:
Iranians and Greeks

Clemen, C., *Fontes historiae religionis Persicae*, Bonn 1920

Clemen, C., *Die griechischen und lateinischen Nachrichten über die persische Religion*, Giessen 1920

Rostovtzeff, M., *Iranians and Greeks in South Russia*, Oxford 1922

Götze, A., 'Persische Weisheit in griechischem Gewande', *Zeitschrift für Indologie und Iranistik* 2 (1923), 60–98; 167–77

Reitzenstein, R.–Schaeder, H. H., *Studien zum antiken Synkretismus*, Leipzig 1926

Reitzenstein, R., *Die hellenistischen Mysterienreligionen*, 3rd ed., Leipzig 1927

Reitzenstein, R., 'Plato und Zarathustra', *Vorträge der Bibliothek Warburg, 1924–5* (Leipzig 1927), 20–37 (now in *Antike und Christentum* (Darmstadt 1963), 20–37)

Windisch, H., 'Die Orakel des Hystaspes', *Verhand. Akad. Wetensch.* 28, 3 (1929)

Christensen, A., *Die Iranier*, in *Kulturgeschichte des Alten Orients* (Handbuch der Altertumswissenschaft III, 1.3) (München 1933), 203–310

Christensen, A., *L'Iran sous les Sassanides*, 2nd ed., Copenhagen 1936

Bidez, J.–Cumont, F., *Les Mages Hellénisés* I–II, Paris 1938

Benveniste, E., *Les Mages dans l'ancien Iran*, Paris 1938

Herzfeld, E., *Iran in the Ancient East*, London and New York 1941

Kerschensteiner, J., *Platon und der Orient*, Stuttgart 1945

Bidez, J., *Eos, ou Platon et l'Orient*, Bruxelles 1945

Richter, G., 'Greeks in Persia', *Am. Journ. Arch.* 50 (1946), 15–30

Festugière, A. J., 'Platon et l'Orient', *Rev. Philologie* 21 (1947), 5–45

Mazzarino, S., *Tra Oriente e Occidente*, Firenze 1947

Cameron, G. G., *Persepolis Treasury Tablets*, Chicago 1948 (*cf. Journ. Near Eastern Studies* 17 (1958), 161–76; *ib.* 24 (1965), 167–92)

Duchesne-Guillemin, J., *Zoroastre*, Paris 1948

Bloch, J., *Les inscriptions d'Asoka, traduites et commentées*, Paris 1950

Goossens, G., 'Artistes et artisans étrangers en Perse sous les Achéménides', *La Nouvelle Clio* 1–2 (1949–50), 32–44

Koster, W. J. W., *Le mythe de Platon, de Zarathustra et des Chaldéens*, Leiden 1951

Tarn, W. W., *The Greeks in Bactria and India*, 2nd ed., Cambridge 1951

Schlumberger, D., 'L'argent grec dans l'empire achéménide', in *Mémoires de la Délégation Archéologique Française en Afghanistan* 14 (1953), 3–64

Festugière, A. J., *La Révélation d'Hermès Trismégiste* I–IV, Paris 1944–54

Ghirshman, R., *Iran from the Earliest Times to the Islamic Conquest*, Harmondsworth 1954

Zaehner, R. C., *The Teachings of the Magi*, London 1956

Osten, H. H. von der, *Die Welt der Perser* ('Grosse Kulturen der Frühzeit'), Stuttgart 1956

Duchesne-Guillemin, J., *The Western Response to Zoroaster*, Oxford 1958

Nenci, G., *Introduzione alle guerre persiane*, Pisa 1958

Harmatta, J., 'Irano-Aramaica. (Zur Geschichte des frühhellenistischen Judentums in Ägypten)', *Acta Antiqua* 7 (1959), 337–409

Bausani, A., *Persia Religiosa*, Milano 1959

Widengren, G., *Iranisch-Semitische Kulturbegegnung in Parthischer Zeit*, Köln 1960

Broadhead, H. D., *The Persae of Aeschylus*, Cambridge 1960

Zaehner, R. C., *The Dawn and Twilight of Zoroastrianism*, London 1961

Wardman, A. E., 'Herodotus on the Cause of the Greco-Persian Wars', *Amer. Journ. Phil.* 82 (1961), 133–50

Somigliana, Ada, *Monismo Indiano e Monismo Greco nei frammenti di Eraclito*, Padova 1961

Duchesne-Guillemin, J., *La religion de l'Iran ancien*, Paris 1962

Altheim, F.–Stiehl, R., *Die aramäische Sprache unter den Achaimeniden*, Frankfurt 1963

Dandamaev, M. A., *Iran pri pervych Achemenidach*, Moskva 1963

Smith, M., 'II Isaiah and the Persians', *Journ. Amer. Orient. Soc.* 83 (1963), 415–21

Frye, R. N., *The Heritage of Persia*, London 1963

Burkert, W., 'Iranisches bei Anaximandros', *Rh. Mus.* 106 (1963) 97–134

Lochner-Hüttenbach, F., 'Brief des Königs Darius an den Satrapen Gadatas', in W. Brandenstein–M. Mayrhofer, *Handbuch des Altpersischen* (Wiesbaden 1964), 91–8

Wilson, R. McL., *The Gnostic Problem*, 2nd ed., London 1964

Widengren, G., *Die Religionen Irans*, Stuttgart 1965

Le Rider, G., *Suse sous les Séleucides et les Parthes*, Paris 1965

Merkelbach, R., 'Die Kosmogonie der Mithrasmysterien', *Eranos-Jahrbuch* 34 (1965), 219–57

La Persia e il mondo Greco-Romano, Accademia dei Lincei, Roma 1966

Walser, G., *Die Völkerschaften auf den Reliefs von Persepolis*, Berlin 1966

Pugliese Carratelli, G., 'Greek Inscriptions of the Middle East', *East and West* 16 (1966), 31–6

Akurgal, E., *Orient und Okzident. Die Geburt der griechischen Kunst*, Baden-Baden 1966

Schwanbeck, E. A. (ed.), *Megasthenis Indica*, Amsterdam 1966

Woelk, D., *Agatharchides von Knidos über das Rote Meer*, Bamberg 1966

Lasserre, F., *Die Fragmente des Eudoxos von Knidos*, Berlin 1966

Colledge, M. A. R., *The Parthians*, London 1967

Nylander, C., '*Assyria grammata*. Remarks on the 21st "Letter of Themistokles"', *Opuscula Atheniensia* 8 (1968), 119–36

Hölscher, U., *Anfängliches Fragen. Studien zur frühen griechischen Philosophie*, Göttingen 1968

Stern, S. M., *Aristotle on the World State*, Oxford 1968

Altheim, F.–Rehork, J. (ed.), *Der Hellenismus in Mittelasien* (Wege der Forschung 91), Darmstadt 1969

Schmidt, E. F., *Persepolis* I–III, Chicago 1953–70

Select bibliography

Fischer, Th., *Untersuchungen zum Partherkrieg Antiochos VII*, diss. München 1970

Altheim, F.-Stiehl, R., *Geschichte Mittelasiens im Altertum*, Berlin 1970

Bielawski, J.-Plezia, M., *Lettre d'Aristote à Alexandre*, Warszawa 1970

Gnoli, G., 'Manichaeismus und Persische Religion', *Antaios* 11 (1970), 274-92

Kahn, C. H., 'On Early Greek Astronomy', *Journ. Hellen. Stud.* 90 (1970), 99-116

Nylander, C., *Ionians in Pasargadae*, Uppsala 1971

Kienast, D., 'Philipp II. von Makedonien und das Reich der Achaimeniden', *Abhandl. der Marburger Gelehrten Gesellschaft*, 1971, 6 (1973)

West, M. L., *Early Greek Philosophy and the Orient*, Oxford 1971

Walser, G. (ed.), *Beiträge zur Achämenidengeschichte* (*Historia*, Einzelschr. 18), Wiesbaden 1972

Burkert, W., *Lore and Science in Ancient Pythagoreanism*, Cambridge, Mass. 1972

Wes, M. A., 'Quelques remarques à propos d'une lettre d'Aristote à Alexandre', *Mnemosyne* 4, 25 (1972), 261-95

Gordon, R. L., 'Mithraism and Roman Society', *Religion* 2 (1972), 92-121

Drews, R., *The Greek Accounts of Eastern History*, Cambridge, Mass. 1973

The Place of Astronomy in the Ancient World, British Academy, London 1974

Metzger, H. and others, 'La stèle trilingue récemment découverte au Létôon de Xanthos', *Comptes Rendus Acad. Inscript.* (1974), 82-93; 115-25; 132-49

Index of Names

Abraham 7, 93
Abtalion, Rabbi 115
Accius 38
Achaeus 23
Acilius, C. 19
Aelian 128
Aemilius Paulus 18, 23, 37
Aeschylus 81, 129–30, 133
Agatharchides of Cnidus 138
Agathocles of Cyzicus 125
Agesilaus, king of Sparta 144
Agricola 57
Aḥiqar 9
Akiva, Rabbi 112
Alcaeus 77–8
Alcimus, Jewish High Priest 106
Alexander the Great 2, 5, 9, 77, 79–80, 108
  and Celts 60
  and Jews 82–3, 94, 98, 111
  and Persians 129, 134–7, 145, 147
  and Romans 16
Alexander the Molossian 14
Alexander Polyhistor 121
Altheim, F. 140
Amasis, king of Egypt 75
Amphicrates of Athens 139
Anaximander 81, 126–7
Andronicus, Livius 17, 20, 91
Antigonus Gonatas 60–1
Antigonus Monophthalmus 43
Antimenides 77–8
Antiochus of Commagene 138
Antiochus III 23, 40, 62, 97–9
Antiochus IV Epiphanes 99–100, 102–7, 109–12, 138

Antisthenes of Rhodes 40–1, 59, 134, 143
Apollodorus of Artemita 139–40
Apollonius 88, 108
Appian 5, 22, 26, 46
Apries 75
Aratus 61
Arenhoevel, Diego 104
Areus, king of Sparta 114
Arganthonius, king of Tartessus 51
Aristeas 76–7, 116, 119
  pseudo-Aristeas 116
Aristobulus of Paneas 84, 93, 103–4, 115–16, 120
Aristos of Salamis 16
Aristotle 4, 13, 85–6
  and Celts 51, 56, 58–60
  and Persians 83, 128, 135–7, 143
  Ps.-Aristotle 59
Aristoxenus of Tarentum 3, 143
Arnaud, Henri 101
Arrian 16, 132, 134, 141
Arsinoe III Philopator 39
Artapanus 116
Artavasdes, king of Armenia 139
Artaxerxes I 98, 125, 137–8
Artemidorus of Ephesus 67, 72
Aseneth, wife of Joseph 117–18
Asoka 7
Astin, A. E. 22
Athenaeus 34, 39, 67, 135, 140
Athenion 33–4
Atossa 28
Attalus I 60, 62
Attalus II 59
Augustine, St 3

169

Index of Names

Index of Names

Index of Names

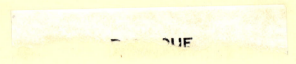